THE
EXTRAORDINARY
ADVENTURES
OF
EOJ NITRAM

JOE MARTIN

978-1-965552-66-7 (Paperback)

BOOKWRIGHTS
HOUSE

admin@bookwrightshouse.com
☎ (213) 286 6700

INTRODUCTION

Eoj Nitram started out as an average kid living in a large family in a poor Brooklyn neighborhood, at an early age things soon changed for the worst. Eoj started to experience a hostile environment that included resentment, anger, frustration and absolute hatred at the hands of the ones he loved most .

You, the reader, are about to embark on a unique tale of how—out of hatred—one man evolved into a psychotic savage with an immense passion for violence and random acts of pure evil.

After many years of his violent reign, Eoj is broken by love and his soul saved from the eternal pits of hell.

This story will also show that with faith the size of a mustard seed, one can go from eternal damnation to eternal life.

Eoj started life in Pineville, Louisiana. The family would relocate to New York and back to Louisiana and back to New York again and settling in New York. Some of Eoj's earliest childhood memories are the simple things like playing outside with his brother's and sister's and cousins, running through the fields, picking berries and discovering a host of bugs, lightning bugs, one of his favorites, also frogs and snakes.

Eoj loved going to school. Riding the bus and talking, playing and laughing with his friends is something he got to do twice a day;

for Eoj this was like therapy, like a reset button restoring his good mood after leaving a hostile place, home. One day on the bus ride to school, Eoj got his first taste of violence at the hands of Henry Martin. Egged on by some friends, Henry decided he would slap Eoj just to see what he would do about it if anything.

After getting slapped—confused and angry—Eoj looked at his uncle, whom also rides the bus with him, as though for advice, and then his uncle said to him, "You better kick his ass or I'm gonna kick yours." That response from uncle was more than enough motivation for Eoj, but before he could react Henry scratched his face so hard that he started bleeding.

Eoj leaped onto Henry and started unleashing a fury of punches, kicks and punches that poor Henry couldn't keep up with Eoj, so he started pleading with Eoj to stop. Feeling just and gratified, he stops. His uncle, still looking at Eoj as if he was from another planet, slowly smiled at him and motioned him to come over to where he was. He then whispered in Eoj's ear saying, "Man I didn't mean to scare you, I would never beat you, I just wanted you to stand up for yourself, good job." "Thanks, unc."

That night at the dinner table his uncle made sure to let the rest of the family know just how brave and strong Eoj was that day. Eoj just sat there smiling and beaming with pride.

The next day on the bus there was no problem with Henry Martin. As a matter of fact, for the rest of the school year the only thing that came out of him was nervous laughter whenever Eoj passed by.

That same summer, one day in the afternoon, there was a great sadness on the faces of the adults in the family. Being children, Eoj and his siblings couldn't figure out what was going on but as far as they were concerned, it wasn't good. Their father had decided to move the family to New York and his word was final, so off to New York the family went. Time to get used to a strange new place and strange new faces. New York didn't last long the first time around.

In New York, Eoj's father worked hard and played just as hard. His wife was truly a housewife with seven children (well 7-to-be, mom was pregnant with twins) to look after and taking care of the household. With his father working half the time and hanging out the other half, things soon took their toll on Eoj's mother. She became depressed and lonely and started to long for her family whom she reluctantly moved from. She soon decided to move back home to Louisiana with all the children in tow.

Once back at her mother's, she decided to find work and get her own place so the children would have the space they so desperately needed to enjoy life. On her own, she found a huge nice house for rent and a nice job as a care taker. Things were starting to go well for Eoj and his siblings. One problem was that the family had a nice big beautiful house without a stick of furniture in it. That soon changed when the grandmother made a phone call on the mother's behalf to the gentleman who owned the furniture store where she got her furniture from and explained her daughter's situation to him.

The owner spoke with Eoj's mother and there was such joy on her face. She said she never heard such kindness: the entire house was going to be furnished with brand new furniture with a payment plan his mom could afford. Oh, happy day.

HERE COMES TROUBLE

Little did Mom know that her plans for a happy life in Louisiana with family and friends were about to be ruined by the man she thought she loved. Mom and the children would soon bear witness to her husband's dark side.

When Eoj's father got word that his wife was doing well without him and had accomplished so much in a short period of time, he flew into a jealous rage and called her and told her that he was coming down to Louisiana to get her and the children and moving them back to New York. This was a true case of "misery loves company".

Mom was devastated, angry, and afraid. Not knowing what to do she broke the news to her family, Eoj and his siblings were confused and quite upset and the adults were equally upset. Eoj's father showed up a day and a half later, a trip that normally took two days, Eoj was starting to notice there was nothing normal about this man he knew as his father.

Back at the house, the furniture truck arrived and just as the guys opened the rear doors of the truck to unload the furniture his mother ran over to greet them and break the bad news to them and just as she started to explain things to them this familiar car with New York plates pulled up behind the truck (talk about perfect timing) and Eoj's father got out with a crazed look on his face, it was the first time Eoj had seen that face and it wouldn't be the last.

Eoj's mother was startled for a moment, he then walked over to her to let her know that we were going to be on the road to New York in a day or two at the most, the man was ice. Eoj's grandmother sent word to his father that he is to stop by at her house with the family before heading back to New York. Two days later, the family stopped by grandma's house en route to New York with tears running down her cheeks and broken hearted she had the task of greeting, trying to comfort, and saying goodbye to her grandchildren all at once, it was more than she could bear.

Finally after somewhat regaining her composure, she spoke to Eoj's father telling him that she didn't understand why he was making such a dramatic move, knowing that her daughter didn't want to go back to New York, and then he said to her, "Madea I love her and I'm going to take good care of her and the kids don't worry." She should have worried.

Getting back to New York took the usual two days, go figure. Back in New York, things changed dramatically. Eoj's father had developed a hairline-trigger short fuse.

Eoj and his siblings witnessed and even became victims to it, one example of many came one day, when the parents were talking a little louder than usual and some of the children came out of the room where they had been playing, Eoj being one of them, to see what it was all about. They realized their parents weren't merely talking but arguing, and then out of nowhere there was a loud smack and they saw their mother fall head first into the metal radiator and suffered a nasty cut across her forehead, she got up slowly bleeding, dazed and eyes full of fear as she looked at the children, there she could see that they were also afraid and crying, all but Eoj, he was staring at his father with great anger in his eyes, wishing he could do something to rectify the situation.

Eoj's father glanced at him, as Eoj stood his ground, the other kids then ran back into the room and closed the door, Eoj braced himself for the worst but then his father started out towards his wife and, out of fear, she ran out of the apartment and, after a moment he gave chase and a couple of minutes later, his father returned by himself and grabbed his jacket and headed out again.

Eoj worried about his mom because she was pregnant with twins and could be hurt badly, after another moment, Eoj set out to look for his mother, he didn't have to go far, after reaching the lobby of the building he called out "Mom!! Mom!!" And then he heard a voice say, "over here." She was hiding under the staircase, still bleeding and still looking fearful, she asked him if his father was still in the apartment. Eoj told her no and that he grabbed his jacket and left. Eoj's mother assured him that she was ok and then they headed back to the apartment.

Once back at the apartment, the other children gathered around their mother showing love and concern for her safety, it was the first time they witnessed violence at the hands of their father. Soon after the incident, mother gave birth to twins and things seemed to be alright for a while and then came the accusations about mom being too friendly with their mutual male friends and his questioning why Eoj was so fair skinned and had curly hair when the rest of family didn't. With all the arguing and violence, Eoj started to act out in school, as well as with a few of his siblings, Eoj also developed a bed-wetting problem from a consistent nightmare he would have, he dreamed that he got up in the middle of the night to use the bathroom and as he started to walk through the living room he heard the floor creek loudly and he also heard a loud growl. Eoj thought it was a huge gorilla waiting to jump on him so he turned around and ran back to his bedroom, too afraid to go through the dark living room by himself, he promptly wet the bed.

In the morning his mother came into the bedroom to wake the kids and get them ready for school, one by one she woke them up and sent them to the bathroom to wash their face and brush their teeth and just as she approached Eoj's bed, she could smell the strong scent of urine and when she saw the large stain, she asked him if he was ok and he said yes, so she took him to the bathroom and washed him and got him ready for school.

When Eoj got home from school, his mother asked him once again if he was ok and he once again said yes, and then she asked him why he thought he wet the bed, and he told her of his bad dream and how the living room was too dark at night. She told him that he'd better get his little ass up and use the bathroom at nights.

Eoj was a little afraid of the way his mother spoke to him and she would soon make the matter worse by using the only answer she knew when she didn't know the answer to a complex situation, a beating. The only person worse than Mom was Dad.

So that night, when Eoj got the urge to go, he got up and headed to the bathroom but as soon as he entered the dark living room he once again heard that same loud creek on the floor, he didn't wait for the growl before making it back to his bedroom and let out a big sigh and got back in bed and thought he'd better sit up the rest of the night and hold it in.

Morning came and Eoj realized that he and the bed were wet, Eoj jumped out of bed and ran to the bathroom but it was far too late. He heard the bathroom door open and close again, and when he turned to look, he saw his mother standing there with a belt; it wasn't such a good morning for Eoj.

On the way to school that morning, his mother informed him that if he wet the bed again, he would get the same treatment. Eoj was out of his mind that day, trying to find a solution to what has now become his biggest problem. Eoj's parents took turns beating him for his bed-wetting problem.

One day in particular, his father woke him one morning and asked him if he had wet the bed, and Eoj, with his head bowed and nearly crying, said, "Yes, dad," and then his father said to him, "when I get home tonight, I'm gonna beat your ass, now go use the bathroom." Eoj then turned and went to the bathroom.

In school that day Eoj couldn't concentrate on anything knowing he was facing an imminent threat when he got home that day. When he reached home, he sought comfort in his mother's arms and he felt safe.

That night at bedtime, he went to the bathroom before going to bed, feeling safe and happy that his father was not home yet, thinking that if he had a dry night, his dad would not keep his promise the next day. Nothing could have been further from the truth.

Later came and it was after 3 a.m. that morning and, in a soft voice, Eoj was awakened by his father telling him to go the bathroom.

Eoj got up immediately and realized his bed was still dry, he smiled and went to the bathroom and, while in there, realized the lights in the living room were on, thinking to himself maybe his dad was going to start leaving those lights on for him.

On his way back to the bedroom he got an eerie feeling that something wasn't quite right. His worst nightmare was standing in the middle of the living room with a large belt wrapped around one of his hands and then said to Eoj, "Didn't I tell you that I was gonna beat your ass when I got home?"

Eoj answered yes, his eyes as wide as saucers and his heart beating out of his chest as fear ripped through his body. His only thoughts were that he was going to die that night and there was no one there to help him. When his father told him to lay across the couch, Eoj desperately started looking around for his mother hoping that she would be somewhere so she could see and hear him, but mom would not be there for him—he would have to face this brute with anger issues by himself.

Wearing nothing but his underwear, Eoj already crying slowly, laid across the couch, his father then did something very strange that scared Eoj even more, his father told him to place his hands behind his back, Eoj—terrified—complied and then his father knelt over him and took one of his knees and placed it on the palm of Eoj's hand, thus pinning both of hands together, and then leaned all of his weight on top of Eoj as he started to sink into the couch. Not quite finished, he took his free hand and placed it on top of the back of Eoj's head and pushed Eoj's face down into the cushion, making sure Eoj's mom wouldn't hear him cry for help.

As the brute started this vicious beating, Eoj realized the obvious, he couldn't breathe or cry out. With every lashing, the brute left a fresh bruise and blood trickling down his legs all the while pushing Eoj's head down into the cushion. No one could hear Eoj, not his mother or his siblings in the next room. Eoj felt himself getting very weak and the brute had yet to let up on the beating, Eoj finally started to fight for his life by jerking his body side to side to throw the brute off balance, it worked, he was crying so hard from the pain that not a sound came out of his mouth.

The brute took one look at Eoj and realized he had gone way too far, now wanting to play nice, he told Eoj to stay put while he went into the bathroom and got a wet towel to wipe off Eoj's injuries. While tending to Eoj, he got him to stop crying, realizing the near killing was over, Eoj slowly got on his feet and started off toward his bedroom, the brute called to him and told him to sit back down on the couch for a minute, so he did and the brute went into the kitchen and after a minute, came back out, walked over to Eoj and offered him a piece of fried chicken that he had been cooking. Eoj's first thought was (you're kidding, right?) but he accepted the offer out of fear, ate it and went to bed.

The next morning when his mother came into the room to get the children up and ready for school, she noticed Eoj sitting up in his bed still looking sad and horrified, so she went over to him and asked him what was the matter and then Eoj flung the covers off his legs to expose his bruised and bloody legs. His mother gasped with horror in her eyes and then asked him if his father did that to him and he said yes.

His mother then realized why Eoj's father closed the bedroom door when he left the room to go check on his chicken, something he never does. Eoj's mom had to keep him home for the rest of the week or there would have been some trouble behind that situation. When his father came home that night, his mother confronted him about the situation and they started arguing to the point where it almost became physical.

For the rest of the week, Eoj was treated like a little prince, no homework, treats, and TV by his mom, but his dad hardly spoke to him, which he didn't seem to mind. When next week came and Eoj was to go back to school, his mother told him not to speak of what happened to him but to give his teacher the note that she was giving him, and if anyone should ask to say that he was sick. When Eoj and his siblings got home from school that day his mother asked him what his teacher said to him after reading the note and he replied that she hopes he feels better.

Mom then prompted the children to start their homework while she went into the kitchen to start dinner. Things weren't getting better for Eoj and his siblings, they still had to contend with the unusual punishments and beatings at the hands of their parents, it seemed the more they argued and fought with each other, the more they took their frustrations out on the children, what little peace there was, was slowly disappearing from their humble home and was quickly becoming a survival of the fittest.

This all started when Dad continued working late nights and then went to hang out with friends afterward, giving Mom and the family little to none of his time. Mom seemed to have tried everything—having a hot tub waiting for him and a hot meal to boot, and the children would all be washed and ready for bed by the time he got home. And to show his appreciation for all her hard work to make time for just the two of them, he would come home, have his home-cooked meal, soak in his hot tub, change into freshly pressed clothing prepared by yours truly, Mom, and then tell the children goodnight. He would tell Mom he would see her a little later and walk right out the front door.

What a slap in the face. Mom's facial expressions told the kids all they needed to know, and they needed to get out of her face and go straight to bed—and that's exactly what they did.

If looks could kill, Eoj's dad would be dead already. Eoj's mom didn't have any friends, and she really needed an adult to speak with about adult situations. The children would be of no help in times like these.

Eoj's mom wouldn't speak to most of the other women in the building; she made it known that she suspected some of them of being up to no good when it came to her husband. She said they would smile at him too long and hug him too hard whenever they ran into him.

Unfortunately, one day her suspicions would prove to be true. Eoj's mom soon met a nice elderly woman who lived on the first floor and had a bird's-eye view of the lobby. As they became closer friends, she would soon give Eoj's mom the scoop on some of the tenants in the building and also speak to her about religion. They developed a strong relationship, and one day the elderly lady told Eoj's mother that she had seen her on the day she ran from her husband and hid beneath the staircase, and asked her if that big man searching for her that day was her husband, and she said yes, he was.

"Well," she said, "I have something to tell you about him, but only if you want to hear it, because I don't like getting involved in people's personal lives, and what I have to tell isn't nice." Then Eoj's mom told her that it was okay, that she could tell her anything. The elderly woman then disclosed that she had seen her husband numerous times, right across the lobby from her, visiting the super's wife when he wasn't there and also a woman on the second floor who happened to be the next-door neighbor. She was shocked but not totally surprised, for this information helped her understand her husband's sometimes suspicious behavior—like when he would say he was going down to see the super about something in the apartment that needed to be repaired (not really) and then be gone for long periods of time, or how he would say he was going out to get some cigarettes and she would never see him leave the building. Now why was that? she thought to herself.

Eoj's dad didn't know it at the time, but he was about to get so busted on both accounts. His wife waited for the perfect time to bust her husband and catch him in the act with both women. She didn't have to wait long until her husband said he was going to see the super about painting a couple of rooms in the apartment that were looking dull. As he left the apartment, Eoj's mom put her plan in place and loosened one of the knobs on the tub until it started to leak. Perfect, she thought to herself. She then went to the front room where the children were watching TV, gave them a snack, and told them she would be right back and that they had better behave themselves.

She then went down the stairs to the super's apartment, a bit scared but more angry than anything else. She knocked on the door. A moment later, the super's wife opened the door with a surprised look on her face, and then Eoj's mom asked if her husband or the super were there. She replied no, and Eoj's mom thanked her and was about to turn and head back upstairs—but then heard her husband call out to her. Surprised, she looked into the apartment; he was coming out of one of the rooms looking suspicious. He asked her what she was doing there.

"Never mind that. Why did she say you weren't here, and where is the super, huh?"

Before he could say anything, she turned and went back upstairs to the apartment and left him there.

A couple of minutes later, he came back to the apartment with rage on his face, went right up to her, and in a loud, angry voice again asked her what the hell she was doing there. She calmly replied, "It so happened, after you left here, I went to the bathroom and noticed the knob on the tub was leaking, so I went downstairs to catch you to add that to the list."

"Bullshit," he said. She told him to go see for himself—and he did, and it was leaking thanks to her.

He then grabbed his jacket and left, off to the bar or pool hall or wherever—not to be seen for the rest of the night.

Eoj's mom had a grin on her face for two reasons:

1. because her plan worked, and
2. she couldn't wait to put her second plan in place and bust him again, now that she had inside info on him thanks to her new friend downstairs with the bird's-eye view of the lobby.

Eoj's mom and dad never spoke about the first incident again because every time she touched on that subject, he gave her a mean look and promptly changed the subject. But she would soon get her chance to bust him a second time, thanks to his lack of consciousness.

The day came when he would take one of his cigarette runs, and she asked him to pick up some sugar also. He said that he would, and off he went—once again without his jacket. Mom went straight to the front window to see if he would come out of the building, and he didn't. She waited a few more minutes and still no sign of him. She then knew he was right next door, and she thought to herself how he could be so brazen and careless to do this—or was it that he just really didn't care?

Mom then took a deep breath and went to the cupboards and took out a cup to "borrow" some sugar next door. She said nothing to the kids this time.

Off she went next door and paused, put her ear to the door to listen, and she heard something she didn't like. She started banging on the door rather than knocking. Things went quiet inside that apartment, and no one answered.

After another moment, she went back inside her apartment and stood by the door, looking out of the peephole. After a few minutes, she spotted her husband coming out of the apartment next door. She started to open the door and once again confront him about his indiscretions, but decided against it because of his temper. Satisfied with what she saw with her own eyes, she kept this one to herself for now.

When he returned, he had his cigarettes, the sugar, and a surprise for her—he also bought her a pack of the cigarettes that she smoked. She looked at him surprised, and he said, "Oh, they were on sale." She thanked him, but she knew his story didn't hold water because that was something he never did for her. But she took it as confirmation that she saw what she saw and would use it against him when the time was right.

Things between the parents didn't get any better; in fact, they slowly got worse and worse, becoming the norm. And when things became too much for Eoj's mom, she went downstairs to consult with her elderly friend. It was good for her because it kept her calm through her storms.

One day, on the way to school, Eoj stepped on a small nail that came through the piece of cardboard he placed in his sneaker to cover the hole in it. The pain was great, but Eoj continued to school despite the pain. By the time he got to his homeroom he was limping and leaving small bloodstains with every step he took. His teacher noticed and asked him to come up to her desk.

Once there, she asked what was the matter, and he told her what happened. She looked at his foot and realized she needed to send him to the nurse's office and give his mother a call. While Eoj was being treated and enjoying a lollipop the nurse had given him, his mother showed up with a new pair of generic sneakers for him.

Eoj gladly put them on, but on the way out of the school he started looking at the other kids' sneakers and noticed that most kids were wearing Pro-Keds, Adidas, and Pumas, etc. But there were a few also wearing the same generic brand as he. His mother noticed how sad he looked, and she told him that one day he would be able to get those same name-brand sneakers. He smiled and said, "Ok, Mom."

Eoj's mom wasn't an educated woman, and neither was Dad. Mom was a housewife and caretaker for her children, and Dad worked maintenance for a bank. So there was only one salary coming in for a family of nine. So yes, they were poor.

And being poor, Eoj and his siblings had to quickly learn to share just about everything. When it came to food, there was no such thing as leftovers. But in the clothing department, you had better luck being a younger sibling, because clothing and shoes were passed down from older to younger. That's just the way things were.

The family really enjoyed the holidays together. Thanksgiving was the great feast and dessert, and Christmas was more of the same, plus gifts for everyone. Those were the best of times.

As time went by, things were changing. One day, Mom was invited to church by her elderly friend from downstairs, so she went with her one Sunday and found herself liking it. Mom thought to herself that it was church that had been missing in her life, and she didn't want to miss it anymore.

But it was quite a different story when it came to Eoj's dad going to church. He reacted negatively and hostile whenever Mom would ask him to join her and the children. The kids, on the other hand, enjoyed making new friends and hanging out with them for a few minutes after services were over. Eoj's dad would eventually use Mom's going to church as the reason for walking out on her and the family one day.

One day, Eoj's mom decided she was going to beat all the children out of frustration for her husband. Unfortunately, this was becoming the norm when she was really upset about something—or nothing; they were one and the same.

Eoj and his siblings were quite tired of it but could do little about it. Eoj wanted out of this situation and decided he would run away this time. So when his mom made them line up as usual, he got on the end of the line as usual, hoping she would wear herself out before getting to him. No such luck. She seemed to be getting a second wind after the fourth victim, and with only two more ahead of him, he turned and started walking toward the front door.

Once there, he quickly started unlocking the locks, and as he opened the door, he heard her scream for him to get back in here. They both knew it was too late for her to catch him, so he kept going—where? Not even he knew. He was just happy to be out of there.

It was still daylight, so he headed toward a familiar playground and deli he knew of. As he got to the deli, he realized he didn't think his little excursion through. Suddenly he had more questions than answers: Where is he going to stay? Who with? What about school the next day? And most importantly—what about food? He was getting hungry; it had been a few hours since he left home.

Well, he knew how to take care of the hunger problem even without money, so he went into the deli to score dinner for the night and worry about tomorrow when it got there. He was able to score dinner: a pack of spiced ham, a pack of cheese, two rolls, a small jar of mayo, chips, a plastic knife, and a soda.

Don't ask—Eoj learned early to be good at what you needed to be good at.

Eoj made his way to an empty bench back at the playground with his score, sat there, made himself two nice sandwiches, and enjoyed his dinner.

Not knowing what to do next, he started walking around the playground. The sun was starting to set, and just as he sat to ponder his next move, he heard a familiar voice say out loud, "There he is, Dad." When he looked up, he saw his older brother in the passenger seat of his father's car, pointing him out to his father, who then stopped and got out of the car and stared at him.

Eoj had never seen that look before, so when his father told him to get his ass in the car, he didn't bother to run. He just walked over to the car and got in, slightly relieved and afraid about what was going to happen next when they got home. Not a word was spoken the whole trip home.

Once home, his mother, although upset with him, asked him if he was okay. He said he was. She then told him to go and get ready for bed. As he was preparing for bed, his father entered the room, walked up to Eoj, and just started to stare at him—not knowing what to do or say.

Eoj looked up at his father and gave a nervous smile, and just as he smiled, his father slapped him so hard.

Eoj was in instant shock, fear, and pain. He stood there holding his jaw because he couldn't close it, and as the brute left the room, Eoj fell to his knees and started to cry loudly—but no one came to his rescue. The brute had just added more coals on top of an already smoldering fire of anger that Eoj held in his heart for him.

In the morning at the table, Eoj could barely open his mouth to eat his breakfast. His mom came into the kitchen and noticed that he hadn't eaten but was instead crying and holding his jaw. Mom took a closer look at him and realized that his jaw was almost swollen shut. She then realized there was no way Eoj was going to school like that.

She started to walk to the bedroom to confront her husband and then remembered he left earlier than usual. Wonder why.

That evening, when Dad got in, he was promptly confronted by Mom. She told him in a loud and clear voice that he could not keep hitting the kids like they were grown adults because they weren't, and that they would get in trouble if she was ever to send one of them to school after he hit them the way he does.

Eoj's dad didn't know how to simply beat the kids, so he just beat them up. If you didn't humble yourself or look like you were hurting enough for Dad, he'd turn up the hurt until you did. Mom was the same way.

One day, Eoj's oldest brother paid the price when he decided he wasn't going to humble himself for the brute during a routine beating because he said it made him look and feel weak. What? So during the beating, Eoj's brother disobeyed a command to hold his hand out for another lash from the thick leather belt his father was using on him. His father taunted him with every lash of the thick belt, knowing he was hurting his son, even grinning before saying, "Come on, hold it out, you can take it."

Eoj's brother was about to cry, and Father knew it, but the oldest son would not give the brute the satisfaction of crying. Instead, he stopped obeying the command to hold out his hand. This infuriated the brute, and he roared at his son, saying, "Hold out your mother-fucking hand right now or I'm gonna stomp a mud hole in your ass!" Eoj, his brother, and the rest of the siblings watching from the other room knew that the older brother had crossed over the point of no return when he still refused to obey even after hearing the threat from the brute. Mom wasn't home, and no one else could help him.

The brute threw down his belt and grabbed his son by the throat. He fought his father off him and then stood straight up as if to challenge his father, and no one was prepared for what happened next.

Next, his father had that look of rage in his eyes and took a full swing at his son, landing a punch squarely into his son's chest. It was so hard and so loud that it sounded like a giant bass drum, and the brute lost his balance and fell to one knee from the force.

All the kids gasped in fear. They all wanted to help the eldest son but couldn't as long as the brute was there. The brute got up from his fall and stared at his son with angry eyes, and his son stared right back at him. After a moment, the brute retreated to his bedroom, and only then did the elder brother show his true feelings. As he slowly sat down on the couch, a tear started down his cheek. Eoj and some of the siblings embraced him, and he cried for a couple of moments before pulling himself together, not wanting the brute to come back out and see him crying.

Eoj's anger and hatred steadily grew toward his father. There was another incident in particular that showed Eoj, his mom, and the rest of the family just how ruthless the brute could be.

He came home really happy one summer day and announced to Mom and the family that he was treating them to a special takeout dinner from his favorite burger joint, Hobie's Home of the Hobo Burger. They were huge burgers, almost like a southern po' boy sandwich. As he started taking orders from the children, he became concerned when one of the smaller ones wanted a hobo burger. You really needed an appetite for that one. He knew the older kids could eat one with no problem but wasn't sure about one of the youngest being able to handle a hobo. So he suggested a smaller-sized burger to the younger sibling so as not to waste money on something she couldn't finish. But Eoj's youngest sister insisted she was starving and would have no problem finishing the hobo burger. The brute grew angry and told her he would get her the burger and that if she didn't eat all of it, he was going to kick her ass.

After hearing that, Eoj already knew it was too late to save his little sister from her doom.

The brute went to get dinner, and upon his return, there were mixed emotions around the table. There were smiles and some sad faces—sad because no one wanted lil' sis to get the beating coming her way.

As the brute and Mom laid out the meal, lil' sis got hers, and the burger looked bigger than her head. Plus she also had fries and a drink she ordered.

As everyone started to eat, the brute reminded her of the consequences if she didn't finish her meal (careful what you ask for). Mom tried in vain to help her by saying she probably didn't know how big the meal would be, but the brute responded that she shouldn't have insisted. Mom just got up and left the table, knowing what would eventually happen to lil' sis, and she didn't want to be there to see it.

Everyone but lil' sis had finished their meal. Seeing this, the brute walked over to her and demanded she finish her meal, but she couldn't. She was already miserable and full. So the brute pulled off his belt, pulled lil' sis from the table, and with no mercy, beat her to the point of throwing up her meal. He then made her clean it up, wash up, and go to bed.

Needless to say, it was a good meal, but no one really enjoyed it knowing what was going to happen to lil' sis that night.

Eoj often wondered to himself why this man was so angry all the time. Even when he was happy about something, it wouldn't be long before something or someone would ruin the moment, and most times it was the brute himself.

This night was the perfect example. The family did enjoy some rare good times with Father. Most summers he would take the family to his favorite getaway, Sunken Meadow Park on Long Island, for a barbecue, the beach, and the playground. Those were good times for the family.

Eoj remembered a couple of his favorite moments at the park. His dad one time burned a whole pack of hot dogs and didn't want to throw them out, so instead he put them on buns, covered the burnt part with ketchup, and passed them out. When Eoj got his and bit into it, after a few chews he spat it out and threw the rest in the trash. Then he heard this big voice call out to him and ask why he threw out the hot dog. Eoj had no problem with his reply.

With his mother looking on, he told his father, "You burnt it." After looking at Eoj for a moment and hearing his wife chuckle, he told Eoj to go and get a burger instead. His wife then told him that he should have known better, and they both had a little laugh over it.

The other thing that Eoj and his siblings enjoyed was the homemade salad dressing that Dad made. It was also great on the burgers.

It was magical times for the kids because when they got home there was only time to wash and go to bed—no beatings tonight.

Truly magical. Those times didn't last long before it was back to the routine ass-whuppings for everybody. It got to the point that if a day passed and you didn't get one, you truly thought something was wrong. (Sad.)

The parents' relationship had become cancerous and nearing its end, between the father's temper, arguments, Mom pressing him to go to church, etc.

Dad finally got to use Mom's going to church and pressing him to join her as his excuse to end the relationship, chalking it up to the church having changed her and that something was wrong with her. The truth is, he was moving in with someone he had met at a bar one night.

Mom was devastated when he told her of his plans to divorce and move out, leaving her to fend for herself and seven children, no education, and no job to boot. WOW!!!

Mom just stared at him, and he could see the great anger in her eyes (if looks could kill). He then told her that they wouldn't divorce right away but that he needed his space to think it through. Fact was, he had no intentions of ever coming back and told her that to calm her down. It worked. Mom and Dad never said anything to the kids, for they would find out the hard way.

Eoj was on his way to the bathroom one day and saw his father in the hallway with a suitcase in one hand and his car keys in the other, heading toward the front door. He didn't realize that Eoj watched him leave for what would be his last time. Eoj started to say something at the last moment just before his father walked out the door but decided against it, realizing this was the way his father wanted to leave. So he let him leave without saying a word.

"What now?" Eoj thought to himself. Well, he would soon find out. After leaving the bathroom to rejoin his siblings in the bedroom they shared, he heard soft crying coming from his parents' bedroom, so he went there instead.

"Mom," he called out in a soft voice.

She answered, "What is it?"

"Are you ok?"

"Yes. Now go back up front. I will be there in a little while."

Eoj realized she wanted to be alone and headed back up front.

After a while, Mom came up front to join the kids. As they gathered around her, she told them the news of Father leaving and that it was going to be just us for a little while. None of the kids seemed terribly upset about it.

Although saddened, there seemed to be some relief also. But Mom had her work cut out for her. First, she had to figure out how she was going to take care of seven kids on her own. She knew she would have to find work also.

Dad helped her out in the beginning, and things were fine for a while, but after a while, his support dwindled down from little to nothing. Mom eventually had to get on public assistance to pull us through.

In the beginning, when Eoj's mom would ask him to go to the store for her, he would come up with every excuse in the book to not go because he was too embarrassed to use food stamps instead of cash at the market.

Eoj's mom figured out a clever way to get him to go to the market: she simply told him that he could buy something for himself when he went to the market for her. And that was all it took. He got to buy all of his favorite snacks and candies. Going to the market for Mom was no longer a problem.

One day, when Eoj stopped at the local bodega for his mother, he saw a new candy bar and was awe-stricken by it because of its name.

It was called the 100,000,00 Dollar Bar by Nestlé. Eoj approached the counter to get a closer look at this thing. He was so fixated on it and wondered to himself how the store owner could possibly afford to have so many of them in the display case all at once at that price.

As he stood there just staring at them, the owner, who knew him, said, "Hi, buddy, see anything you want?" And Eoj, with a saddened look, said to the owner, "Yes, but I can't afford it." Then, with a smile, the owner asked him what he wanted, and Eoj said that he wanted the 100,000,00 bar. The owner's smile grew wider, realizing what Eoj was thinking, and his smile turned into a chuckle and then a small laugh—then a bigger laugh.

Eoj looked up at the owner and realized that he had tears coming down his face and was having a hard time catching his breath. Finally the owner said to Eoj, "I tell you what, today's your lucky day. I'm going to give you one for free."

Eoj said, "Really?"

With a big smile on his face, the owner said to him, "Trust me, kid, you earned it," and handed him the candy bar he so admired. As he left the store, waving goodbye, he could still hear remnants of laughter. It took him a few minutes to figure out what had just happened, and when he did, he just smiled and took another bite of his new favorite snack. (Sometimes ignorance is bliss.)

Mom started going to church more often and acquired some new friends, some in situations similar to hers. The women's favorite pastime became church, visiting one another, having a good meal, and of course talking about everything under the sun.

School was becoming more difficult for Eoj, not because he couldn't do the work, but because ever since his dad left he was losing interest in it. He didn't care to do it anymore and was becoming more of a free spirit.

He desperately needed an outlet from the routine, and one day after school, he stopped at the little bodega on the corner where he got his favorite snacks and asked the owner for a part-time job. The owner was impressed that a kid as young as Eoj would choose to work after school rather than watch TV or go to the playground and hang out. But his store was a small one, and there wasn't enough work for him to hire Eoj.

The bodega owner saw that Eoj was saddened and that he really wanted to help him out. He also felt that Eoj would be a good worker, so he told him, "Listen, if you are serious about working, I will ask my son—who owns the supermarket around the corner—to give you a job there. But there are some conditions."

Eoj smiled wide and inquired about the conditions. He said to Eoj that he had to do well in school and do his homework, as well as obey his parents—in this case, obey his mom—and most importantly, only if his mom said he could work.

Eoj promised to do all the things asked of him and said he would speak to his mom about it as soon as he got home, and would be back the next day with her answer. The owner asked him to bring his mom with him, and Eoj said that he would, then left for home.

Once home and overcome with joy, he rushed over to his mom and explained everything to her, and she happily agreed. Eoj had a hard time sleeping that night.

The next morning, while sitting at the table having breakfast, his mom reminded him of his promise and then told him to come straight home after school and they would go to the supermarket together. Eoj gave a big smile as he left for school. Things went well in school that day, and his teachers were pleasantly surprised that he actually engaged and got some work done that day.

Once home, he found his mother ready and waiting for him. She said, "Ok, let's go."

When they got to the supermarket, they found that the owner and his wife were expecting them, and after the introductions, the owner explained to Eoj and his mother what his duties, hours, and salary would be and asked if they agreed with them. They did. Then the owner said, "See you tomorrow," and thanked Eoj's mom for bringing him, and she in return thanked him and his wife for giving Eoj the opportunity to be a little more independent, which would also help him mature more and become a responsible young man.

Eoj said nothing on the way home. Beaming with pride, he let his unbreakable smile do all the talking. Back home, he was more than motivated to do his homework and get ready for the next day. It was going to be a big day for him.

When the next day came, Eoj awoke with a big smile on his face and full of energy. He ate breakfast, said goodbye to his mom, and hurried out the door, making the day a good one. After school, he ran all the way to his new job. Once there, his boss greeted him with a firm handshake and gave him his first assignment. Eoj finished the task promptly and reported back to his boss for his next task. His boss looked surprised and went with Eoj to check over his work, and when he saw that it was all done correctly, he said to Eoj with a smile on his face, "Wow, you're better and much faster than the last guy who used to work here. If you keep this up, we are going to get along just fine."

He then said to Eoj that he earned himself a short break before moving on to his next job. "You can grab yourself a snack and drink and relax for ten minutes." Eoj thought to himself, I must be in heaven—this is the best job ever.

As time passed, he settled into the job nicely—they were a perfect fit. When he got his first paycheck, he couldn't believe his eyes. He could barely contain himself. His first thought was to share part of his check with mom and to treat his siblings to dessert.

When he got home, dessert in hand and some much-needed cash for mom, they made him feel like a hero, and he liked it. He felt even more motivated to continue to work and help out.

One day, Eoj decided to treat some of his brothers to lunch at the neighborhood McDonald's after playing in the park. After leaving McDonald's for home, Eoj and his brothers were blindsided by a couple of robbers who, unbeknownst to them, had been following them for blocks. Then they decided to make their move. One of the perps came up behind Eoj and put him in a choke hold, and the other pulled out a gun and told Eoj's brothers not to move as he went through Eoj's pockets and took what was left of his paycheck.

After it was over, Eoj was angry but glad no one got hurt. It was the first and the last time anyone ever robbed Eoj without consequences. When he saw that his brothers were still in shock, he made light of the situation by saying that if those guys were smart, they would have robbed him before and not after they left McDonald's—and left it at that. His brothers smiled with him as they headed home.

Once home, his brothers rushed over to their mother to tell her what happened to them and how calm Eoj was during what they told her was a very scary event to them. His mother then asked him if he was ok, and if they called the police. Then she asked the eldest son why he didn't do anything. Eoj then told his mother that there was nothing anyone could have done, so that's what they did to get through it. His brothers shook their heads in agreement. Then mom calmed down and told them to please stay in for the rest of the day.

Eoj, although cool and calm on the outside, was hiding a smoldering rage inside and couldn't understand why he had such a strong desire for revenge. Eoj and his brothers got their first taste of just how cruel and unforgiving the outside world could be that day.

Back at work, Eoj never mentioned what happened to his boss, who was like a father figure to him, and he didn't want him to worry over what he considered to be nothing. Eoj was starting to let that desire for revenge get the best of him. When he got his next paycheck, he went back to McDonald's on a Saturday at about the same time he and his brothers were there the previous Saturday, to see if any of the guys who robbed him would show up. While sitting there, he realized he had bad intentions—he was actually hoping and wishing that one of these guys would show up so he could punish them. But at the same time, he realized he never got a good look at either of the guys because they attacked him from behind. So he just got up and headed home, still feeling the need to avenge himself.

Once back home and watching TV with his siblings, he was able to calm himself. Eoj was always like that—wanting to take care of his conflicts without involving anyone unnecessarily.

At a time when Dad wasn't helping out much, Mom announced that the family was going to have to move because they could no longer afford the apartment without Dad's help, which also meant new schools and faces to get used to. Mom, with the help of some of her church sisters, soon found a nice apartment for the family, and it was not too far from the previous place.

It turned out the family moved into the same building as one of Mom's close friends. She had kids around the same age group as Eoj and some of his siblings. It wasn't long before the kids became friends and started getting into mischief. Eoj and his siblings had to quickly adjust to new schools and new grades. Junior high school would be one of Eoj's biggest challenges.

Eoj had to give up the job he loved so much because schoolwork had become too demanding, and he could no longer do both. Making friends at the new school was also hard. Most kids took Eoj's humble beginnings for a weakness—and Eoj was anything but, as some students would soon find out the hard way. With no job as an outlet and not being able to help his mom out as before, he started to become a frustrated and angry young man.

One day, after being held up in class because the teacher wanted to see him to discuss his lack of interest in his work and homework, Eoj was giving the teacher a hard time and didn't want to talk about it. After about ten minutes of refusing to talk, the teacher said they would discuss it another time and dismissed Eoj for lunch. Realizing he was running late and might not make it to lunch, he started to run to ensure he would make it. But on his way down the staircase, a much bigger student blocked his way and asked him if he was a freshman. Before he could answer, the brute demanded, "Give me your money, you little mother******," and started to pat his pockets searching for money.

Eoj, afraid and angry, refused to be the brute's victim. As the brute was searching his pockets, Eoj stepped back, and just as the brute reached for his pocket again, Eoj swung with all his might, and his fist made solid contact with the brute's jaw. BAM!! Down the brute went, sprawled out on the staircase.

Eoj thought to himself, Wow, that felt good and empowering. He liked the feeling—then quickly thought he'd better get out of there before someone saw him and he got into more trouble. But as he started to run, he stopped and decided to rob the brute for making him miss lunch. He quickly went through his pockets— and jackpot: $70 for his troubles.

Eoj skipped the lunchroom and went straight to the little diner and treated himself well. Back at school in his homeroom, there was a knock on the door. The teacher got up and opened it. It was the principal—and the brute. Eoj already knew what the visit was about. The principal let the brute walk around the room, and when the brute came to Eoj's desk and just stood there, Eoj looked up at him and stared, giving him a look as if to say, Go ahead. I dare you.

The principal walked over and asked the brute, "Is this the guy?" The brute said no, and then he and the principal left the room. Some of the students looked at Eoj in awe because they could tell why the brute didn't identify him—he was afraid of him. And Eoj was loving it. He was proud of himself for standing up for himself and also knowing the brute would now think twice before coming after him again.

Eoj, being new at this particular junior high school, would soon again have to defend himself and send a clear message that if you were going to come after him, it wasn't going to end well for you.

One particular day, Eoj was sitting at the front of the class taking notes for homework when, all of a sudden, a deep, loud voice coming from the back of the class said, "Hey, move your bleeping head!" After repeating the message a couple of times, a large ring with about thirty or more keys on it flew past Eoj, just missing his face.

Eoj turned around to see a large, angry-looking guy walking toward him. Not sure what to do, he just waited to see what this brute was up to. The brute walked past Eoj, picked up the keys that had landed in front of his desk, and without any warning—wham!—punched Eoj in the eye so hard that he flipped backward out of his chair/desk and hit the floor. In shock and in great pain, he was fearful and confused, but he still had the presence of mind to know he needed to flush his eye with cold water to keep the swelling down. As he got up to leave, he heard the teacher say, "Don't start any trouble," as he walked out of the room.

After finding a water fountain, he flushed his eye, and although swollen, it was minimal. Now feeling like an outraged inferno, he headed back to class, thinking of the best way to take care of this brute. Once back in class, Eoj noticed the brute had taken his seat, thrown all his books on the floor, and was giving him the "I dare you" look. Just as Eoj started toward the brute, the teacher once again told him not to start anything and to take a seat in the back of the class. The brute had a grin on his face that Eoj couldn't wait to wipe off.

As he sat in the back of the class, anticipating his next move, a couple of students he knew looked at him bewildered, as if to say, Are you going to let this guy get away with that? Eoj motioned to them not to worry.

Suddenly, a sinister grin came across his face—he had his next move, a move that would let the brute know he was messing with the wrong guy at the right time. As the teacher had her back to the class writing notes that were to be copied, Eoj made his move. He picked up his chair/desk unit and put it over his shoulder, thinking to himself, Man, this is a little heavy, but he couldn't wait to see the look on the brute's face after he smashed it over his head.

Slowly, Eoj crept toward the clueless brute. As he passed his two friends, their eyes became wide as saucers because they couldn't believe what they were seeing. The teacher still had her back to the class—perfect, Eoj thought to himself. He got behind the brute and brought the desk/chair down on his head with such force that it sounded like a car crash. The whole classroom erupted with gasps and screams. The teacher was in shock, and the brute was out cold. Once she regained her composure, she sent Eoj to the principal's office. He left the room to thunderous applause from the students.

At the principal's office, Eoj tried to explain the situation, but after hearing the part where Eoj slammed the chair/desk down on the guy's head, the principal had a look of horror on his face and gave Eoj a two-week suspension from school. Mom wasn't too happy to hear that when he got home. Eoj couldn't care less at that point— he was glad he gave the brute just what he deserved, and the two-week suspension was just a bonus.

During his time off from school, Mom didn't make it easy on him, giving him chores to do and very little TV time. Eoj didn't mind these things because he knew how to bide his time. He enjoyed the time he had to himself and by himself. Eoj was a thinker, always creating things in his head.

After returning to school from his suspension, it was just about lunchtime, so Eoj headed straight to the lunchroom to find the line very long. Just as he was deciding whether to get on it, he looked up to the front—and as fate would have it, the brute responsible for his suspension was next in line to be served. At that moment something came over Eoj, and he headed straight toward the brute.

Just as he reached him, the brute had received his lunch. Eoj promptly grabbed his tray and said, "Give me that, you punk!!"

The brute was in shock but quickly released the tray. Eoj stared at him for a moment, hoping there would be a disagreement—there wasn't—so Eoj walked over to a table. A few students got up to give him a seat. He sat and enjoyed the brute's lunch while also enjoying this new feeling of empowerment. It was both gratifying and profound.

For the next two weeks, the brute tried to befriend Eoj to no avail. Finally, one day, the brute, unwilling to give up, saw his opportunity when Eoj was sitting by himself in the lunchroom. He quickly walked over with his hand held out for Eoj to shake. After a brief, hard stare, Eoj shook it, ending the beef between them.

Eoj had a few more incidents in that school before the year was up—victorious in all of them—boosting his confidence and his newly found skills even more.

Back at home, things for the family weren't getting any better. It seemed everyone was going wayward and doing their own thing. The family had to move once again, and there was a new school year to begin. Mother had just found out that the reason the man she was still married to had stopped sending financial support was because he decided to buy a house with the other woman—after refusing a gift house from his father that could have helped keep his family together. To make matters worse, he was treating the other woman's children far better than his own.

After sharing that news with Eoj and the rest of his siblings, Eoj's rage grew even more. When the new school year started, no one in the family was able to handle it well. Still reeling from the news about the brute and his newly chosen family, it was a bad year all around. Mother was angry and didn't know what to do next. The three oldest siblings—who were in high school, Eoj included—started to do poorly and began skipping school altogether. The four youngest ones were still doing okay.

After coming home one day from skipping school, Eoj overheard his mother and older brother discussing how the family would stay afloat with no real income coming in. His older brother concluded that he would just go out and get a job and finish school a little later—never mind that he was only one year from graduating.

Mom put up a fuss at first and then gave in when she realized how much the family really needed the support. Little did she know that Eoj would soon follow suit, knowing they had to put things on the back burner for now and go into full-blown survivor mode. So that's what they did, without any regrets.

The eldest brother found work at a supermarket, and not long after, so did Eoj at another market. They started to do well for themselves and the family, but between the rent and the rest of the bills, things were still a little rough. They were trying to figure out a way to cut costs.

One night, the elder brother was being locked in for the night at his job—he had the graveyard shift of maintenance and restocking the shelves. He noticed one particular night that after locking him in, they also went to check the receiving gate. The elder brother just happened to be on the other side as they checked the gate and noticed he could get a three-to-four-inch gap on the gate when it was locked. After a while, he found a crowbar by the gate and gave it a try. Sure enough, he was able to get the gate up while it was locked.

Later that night, the elder brother called home to speak to Eoj and explain the situation, asking if he wanted to give it a test drive. Eoj agreed, and they set a time for him to be at the gate and tap on it so the elder brother would know it was him.

The first thing the elder brother slid out to Eoj was a couple of pre-made shopping bags to carry the goods. There were steaks, candy bars, batteries, etc. The test run went well, and the next day at the job no one was the wiser. So whenever the family needed some extras, it was just a phone call away.

Eoj worked at a much larger store that had two loading docks, and he worked the overnight shift a few days a week. He could do the same thing on his end—but only when one of the drivers was too lazy to dock a trailer straight, which happened two to three times a week. Between the two brothers, the grocery bill was cut by 80%.

One day, Eoj figured that if he took another full-time job during the day, he could save some money and get his family ahead in life. It wasn't long before he found something closer to doing what he actually liked—driving. Eoj found a job at a coach-builder company; they built custom made-to-order limousines and other made-to-order cars. Great job, Eoj thought to himself. He really loved driving these special cars.

But having two full-time jobs was starting to catch up with him. After about two weeks on the new job, he showed up wearing the uniform from his overnight job—and everyone noticed except him. He was surprised when his new boss asked how long he had been at the other job, and before he could answer, the boss pointed out the uniform he was wearing.

Eoj sighed and explained his situation, and his boss took pity on him and told him to take the day off, adding that he might have something nice for him—but he would have to give up the other job.

Eoj agreed to go home and got his rest. The next morning, his boss told him about his partner who lived in the city and who just happened to be looking for a full-time driver for himself and his family. The job would pay a good deal more than his present job. With the new job, Eoj was able to help the family out a great deal more. But they were moving again. Shortly after moving to the new place, Mom got homesick and informed the family that she was going back south. Some took it hard, and others were okay with it. Everyone was older now and could fend for themselves. Some stuck together, and others moved on.

Eoj had a good job and got his first apartment to himself—a spacious two-bedroom. He liked his space and had extra room in case one or more of his siblings came for a visit. Eoj enjoyed his newly found serenity, but soon discovered he had too much time alone with his anger and frustrations. He needed to find some physical therapy to keep his mental health stable. Remembering those incidents in school, he sought after something he seemed to have a natural talent for: fighting. This would be a new beginning for Eoj.

Eoj found the first of several boxing gyms he would train at. But after the first few months, the training started to take its toll on him. He had to find something closer to work or home. His new gym was in downtown Brooklyn, easy to get to after work and easy to get home from after training.

Eoj loved his new gym and was starting to shine as an up-and-comer. Each sparring match was better than the one before—sending amateurs to the hospital and the pros home with their heads down in shame. Something was starting to happen with Eoj. He was becoming more deadly with every sparring match and even began wearing a sinister grin before, during, and after his matches. It quickly got to the point where the amateurs wouldn't spar with him, and the pros became intimidated and reluctant.

There were some trainers and managers who kept an eye on Eoj during his training, and they had mixed reviews about him. Some of the trainers thought Eoj was already far too dangerous and wouldn't go too far before being barred from the sport for his over-aggressive demeanor. They felt he had too much bloodlust that would soon be out of control. A couple of the managers, however, loved what they saw in Eoj and were more than willing to sign him to a contract because all they saw was dollar signs. Whoever got to sign Eoj knew they would have to get him to tone down his aggression (how ironic) and try to win his fights without killing his opponents.

It wasn't long before one of the managers vying for Eoj approached him and introduced himself.

"Hello, my name is Jaye Diamond, and I would like to discuss signing you to a contract."

Eoj at first just stared at him, but then asked, "How soon can I fight?"

Mr. Diamond replied, "Two months—one month to restructure your fight plan and one month to get you your first few fights and on your way to a championship bout."

Eoj agreed, and Mr. Diamond said he would draw up the contract and they could sign over dinner in a week, and that Eoj could have a lawyer go over the contract if he wanted. Then Eoj asked Mr. Diamond, "Are you a man of your word, sir?"

He said yes, and Eoj gave him a stern look and said, "So am I, so we shouldn't have a problem." The two men shook hands.

While Eoj was taking time off from the ring to go over restructuring his game plan, he visited the gym just to watch the guys spar and work on their fighting skills.

As Eoj was watching the other fighters, one of them walked over to him and said, "Hey, how you doing?"

Eoj said, "What's up?" The stranger then said, "So, I hear you're turning pro."

Eoj just stared at him for a moment, and just before he could answer, the stranger said, "I'm sorry—where are my manners? My name is John Stone. Nice to meet you."

They shook hands.

"Eoj Nitram, nice to meet you," Eoj replied.

"Boy, that's a unique name you got there."

Eoj replied, "Thanks. The first time I heard it, I was confused, but I liked it because I had never heard of anyone else with the name."

John replied, "It's unique, alright."

Eoj looked puzzled and then asked John, "How did you know I was turning pro?"

John said, "Are you kidding me? It's all over the gym. That's all anyone is talking about, and most of the guys want to come to your first fight if you give them the info. I just came up to you personally to ask you myself. I just want to see you take out your first victim."

"What makes you think he's going to be a victim?"

"Yo, Eoj, I've noticed you since your first sparring match, and I've never seen anyone with the kind of raw talent, speed, and skill that you possess. I mean, have you even noticed that the amateurs will not spar you under any circumstances, and the pros avoid you like the plague because they don't want their careers to end before they begin? You're a natural—perhaps even a supernatural. I mean it, I'm a fan. Hey, listen, Eoj, if there's ever something I can do for you, just say the word."

"I just may take you up on that."

"It's an open invitation," John replied. "Catch you later."

"Later," Eoj replied.

As Eoj was leaving the gym, one of the trainers came over to him and said, "I see you've met Mr. Wall Street, and it seems he's taken a liking to you."

Eoj gave the trainer a stern look and then asked, "Do I look like someone's pet?"

The trainer was taken aback and quickly asked Eoj not to take his comment the wrong way. "I just meant that guy never speaks to anyone, and the last time he held a conversation that long, he invested in that guy and made him very rich. You see, Mr. Wall Street is a boxing fanatic and is always looking for fighters with talents other than boxing. That last guy was an inventor and was just about to quit the fight game, fed up with not being able to make enough money to produce his product. He and Mr. Wall Street got to talking one day, and six months later he was cleaning out his locker, saying he didn't have to fight anymore, thanks to Mr. Wall Street."

"That's a great story, but fighting is all I know and all I seem to love right now."

"Well, it must be your boxing skills that have him so intrigued. Maybe he's seeking some pointers from you."

Eoj then asked, "Is he not a good fighter?"

"Not even close," the trainer said. "I think he's just going through a phase and is doing boxing to satisfy his ego. He keeps asking to fight the pros here, but he's nowhere near ready to go up against any of them. Damn, he could barely handle the amateurs on a good day. I guess we'll see how far he'll go if you take him under your wing."

"I guess we'll see," Eoj replied.

The next day, Eoj arrived at the gym early to watch some sparring matches. This sport was in his blood, making it extremely hard for him to be away from the action.

As Eoj was approaching the gym, he noticed a beautiful Rolls-Royce passing by him and stopping in front of the gym. A familiar face got out—it was John Stone (aka Mr. Wall Street)—and Eoj thought to himself, *not bad*.

Eoj went up to the gym, where he then saw Mr. Stone preparing to spar. Mr. Stone spotted Eoj and motioned for him to come over. Once there, he asked Eoj to watch his match and let him know what he thought about it at the end.

Eoj replied, "Sure, no problem."

Once the match was over, some of the guys were laughing and whispering among themselves. John then asked Eoj to give it to him straight, and Eoj replied, "You're overthinking it, which is causing you to take unnecessary punishment."

John then asked what he would have done differently.

"Everything," Eoj snapped, and then said in a stern voice, "I'd much rather break a man's will, wreck his body, and scar his soul. You know—a good, slow suffering."

With his eyes wide as saucers, John said to Eoj, "We're from two different worlds."

Eoj replied, "No doubt. Hey, my next match, I'll show you how it's done."

"Deal," said John.

Eoj then advised John to be wary of some of the trainers there and told him they might try to feed him a pro when he wouldn't be ready for one.

"Will do," John replied, and then asked Eoj if he'd like to get a drink or grab a bite. Eoj looked at his watch and said, "Sure."

As they got to John's car, the driver got out to let them in. He seemed to act a bit timid, and John thought to himself, *That's strange.* At the restaurant, they talked about various things, but mostly the fight game. Eoj informed John that he would be turning pro in a matter of weeks and that he was just waiting on his contract.

John congratulated him and said he couldn't wait for his first fight, and Eoj replied likewise.

As they headed back to the car, Eoj told John that he would make it home on his own and said good night. As John was being driven home, his driver made a comment about Eoj, saying how Eoj gave him the chills and that he couldn't put his finger on it, but there was something about him.

John said, "Yes, I know."

A few weeks later, Eoj had signed his contract and was preparing for his first pro fight. He had chosen the ring name "Marksman" for himself. Little did he know that he would be fighting the national heavyweight champion—undefeated at 15–0—a 250 lb brute from upstate New York.

Eoj's fight weight was 215 lbs, and now training at a private facility on Long Island that his manager owned. During training, Eoj sent all four of his sparring partners to local hospitals, suffering from bone fractures and concussions—unheard of in the history of the sport.

Needless to say, none of them ever came back, no matter how much was offered to them. Eoj's manager and a couple of the trainers quickly realized that Eoj had evolved into a much more deadly talent than they had imagined. Meanwhile, John Stone accepted a sparring match with a deadly pro, unaware of the pro's jealous nature and his intentions of making John the poster boy for being ill-equipped to handle pros.

Needless to say, John was sent to the hospital with a broken body and a crushed ego to boot. Eoj coincidentally stopped by the gym the day after to invite John to sit ringside at his first pro fight, but instead got the news about John and made his way to the hospital. Once there, he couldn't believe his eyes—John was unrecognizable.

Eoj spoke to John briefly and promised him that he would have his day of vengeance, and a steak-and-champagne dinner to celebrate the occasion. John smiled and nodded his head in agreement. Eoj's next order of business was to break the ice and get his first fight under his belt as a win.

The day of the fight, still no word from his manager. He knew when and where to be—good thing, because time was getting tight—so Eoj decided not to wait anymore and drove himself four hours upstate with time to spare.

When he met up with his manager before going to the ring, he was informed that his manager had been robbed of his cash and phone and didn't know Eoj's address by heart. "No problem," Eoj replied. "Let's get this done." Then Eoj informed him that he had nothing against the corner men the manager picked to work the fight, "But I don't need or want them there. That being said, I don't want them serving me or giving me advice. Tell them to just be there and just watch the fight. I know how this looks and sounds, but I just need it to be this way. Thanks."

When told, the men were shocked, saying it was a first, but they understood.

It's fight time, and the men are in the middle of the ring receiving their final instructions before the bell. The bell sounds and Eoj lands a thunderous right to his opponent's jaw, and down he goes. He gets up, barely beating the ten-count, realizing his jaw was broken. Now looking shocked and confused, he tries to keep his distance from Eoj—and he does—until the last seconds of the round, when Eoj rushes him and lands another thunderous right to the body. Just by his reaction, Eoj knew he had cracked his rack (broke a rib), and Eoj gave him a sinister grin as they headed to their corners.

Once there, Eoj just stood waiting for the bell, and so did his corner men. His opponent's team was trying to get him to throw in the towel, realizing that Eoj was way too much for him and that it would only be a matter of time before he wouldn't be able to leave the ring under his own power. But the young champion had too much pride—and not enough sense—to realize what he was doing, although he felt it deep in his heart.

The bell sounds for round two, and Eoj walks right up to his opponent. Before the guy could put his hands up, Eoj unleashes a barrage of body and head shots and he goes down again—slower to get up this time. As he struggles to get to his feet, Eoj stares and stalks him, and the ref sends him to a neutral corner. After giving the all-clear, Eoj rushes in with another tremendous left hook to the temple, delivering a cold, calculated concussion that ends the fight—and a career.

After being rushed by reporters, Eoj reluctantly dealt with them, even though he knew some would ask the most dumb and obvious questions. First question: "Do you think the best man won?" "No doubt," Eoj replies. Next: "Why do you think your opponent lost so badly?" "He had no passion or commitment for the sport. I, on the other hand—when I commit, I go all in, and when I go all in, I go all out. No more questions!" Eoj yells, and walks away.

The next day, Eoj gets word that his opponent died while in a coma and is summoned to the state athletic commission office for drug tests and an interview. After being cleared of any foul play and receiving a stern warning that his career would be over if something like this happened again, Eoj nods and then leaves. Once on the street, there's a crowd of reporters waiting for him. He makes a break for it and gets a cab out of there.

He sits back in his seat and lets out a sigh of relief, and just then his phone rings. It's John—he wants to meet for lunch. Eoj agrees, "But nowhere public," Eoj says. John agrees and says, "I'll send my driver for you." "Ok, cool," Eoj replies.

A short time later, they arrive at the East Side heliport. Eoj then asks the driver, "Exactly where are we going?" The driver responds, "To Mr. Stone's East Hampton estate."

As the helicopter descends, Eoj gets a bird's-eye view of the property and says to himself, *Nice*. John greets him at the door and they go into a large living area and have a seat.

"Drink?" John asks.

Eoj says, "Johnny Blue, a shot of diet coke, and a twist of lime, thanks."

After receiving his drink, Eoj asks John when he got out of the hospital, and John asks Eoj what the hell happened that night in the ring.

The men, drinks in hand, talked for hours about the past, present, and the future. At one point, John says to Eoj, "I hope you don't let what happened discourage you from getting back in the ring."

"Hell no," Eoj replies. "I'd fight tomorrow if I had another victim lined up—um…I mean opponent."

"Don't apologize. You had it right the first time."

"I know, I just didn't want to sound disrespectful. There's something in me that must destroy every challenger, because I could never have an opponent standing over me claiming victory."

John then says to Eoj, "I knew I liked you. We should discuss plan B, because you don't quite see it yet."

"And what is that?" Eoj asks.

John says, "We both know there's a good chance you may kill the next guy also, and then you won't be able to fight anymore—not legally, anyway—and I know you don't want to stop your career just because a couple of lesser men couldn't handle your best."

"That's true, I didn't think of that."

"Yes, let's figure out plan B," John agrees, and says to Eoj, "Why don't you stay here if you want, until your manager gets you your next fight and we figure out plan B."

"Ok, cool," Eoj replies. "I can get used to a place like this."

Over the next few days, Eoj met with his manager to discuss things. His worst fears about Eoj were coming true—he had evolved into such a savage that already his career was in jeopardy. His skills, speed, and strength were far too much for the fighters of his era. Eoj was well ahead of his time, and his manager warned him that if he didn't adjust and slow down, his career would be over in a very short time.

Eoj replies, "So be it. I'm already bored of these so-called pros. A change would be a good thing."

Eoj's manager then told him when his next fight would be. "And FYI," he said, "this guy fights dirty."

"Thanks," Eoj said. "I'll see you at the fight."

"Ok, see you there," the manager replied, and the men parted ways.

It's fight night, and you could feel the excitement in the air. Eoj had avoided the press and public since his first fight and had the press barred from his locker room for this fight.

His opponent was a 6'2", 290-pound hulk of a man. Eoj seemed to get excited after seeing this guy. When coming to the center of the ring for final instructions, you could see how the guy towered over him. Eoj was only 5'8" and 215 lbs. That's what made Eoj so exciting to watch—so much power, speed, and talent in a relatively small package for a heavyweight.

While receiving their instructions, the hulk-like figure looks at Eoj with a smirk on his face as if to say *this guy really?* Eoj kept a straight face and blank stare like a killer white.

The bell sounds to start round 1. The two men rush and meet center ring. Eoj gets off the first punch, a missile-like body shot, and drops the big man to one knee as he lets out a loud grunt as the crowd cheers loudly as the big man took the eight count.

After the count, he charges at Eoj but receives more punishment, a repeated body shot and a dizzying uppercut, and while falling to the canvas he tries to hold on to Eoj but receives another deadly combo—a straight left jab and a right hook to the jaw—and down he goes for the second time. He barely gets up before the ten count and is then saved by the bell.

Looking confused, angry, and relieved all at once, he stumbles back to his corner with a variety of damage done to him in the form of a broken nose, severely swollen jaw, and some bad body bruising.

The big guy's team was just as shocked as the big guy and didn't know what to do next, and as one of his team members tried to throw in the towel, he was punched right off the ring apron. Then the big guy yelled for his whole team to get out of his corner, and just then, Eoj looked down at ringside at his manager and John Stone, signaling the end for the big guy.

The bell sounds for round 2. Eoj rushes over to the big guy's corner just as he gets off the stool and lets into him with a barrage of body and head shots. He's landing 3 and 4 punches before the big guy can react to one. He's doomed as Eoj continues the onslaught of vicious combos, and the big guy lets out a loud cry of pain. Eoj slows the pace to one crippling punch at a time—body then head repeatedly—and the big guy can no longer protect himself as his corner cries out for the ref to stop the fight. The ref looks things over but hesitates, and now it's too late. With one last devastating blow to the head the big guy goes down for good, and Eoj leaves the ring immediately and heads to his locker room followed by his manager and Mr. Stone. The crowd is in a frenzy over what they've just witnessed.

Meanwhile, Eoj and Co. were headed to the roof of the building escorted by management and security. Mr. Stone explained to Eoj that he had foreseen this coming and so planned accordingly. Eoj nodded his head as they got into the helicopter.

Eoj's manager handed him an envelope with a check and a torn contract and said, "No hard feelings huh?"

Eoj responded, "None at all."

Mr. Stone then asked Eoj's manager, "Can we drop you at the East Side heliport?" He said, "Yes, thanks," and then turned to Eoj and said, "Let's wait and see what happens to this guy before you make your next move, I'd like to be there for support ok?" And Eoj thanked him as he got out at the heliport.

Mr. Stone then asked Eoj if he wanted to stay in the city or country for the next few days.

"Country, thanks man."

"I'm sure we're going to have to initiate plan B soon and we should start going over it."

"Cool, let's get it done."

The next morning, Eoj got the call he was expecting. The big guy was near death and not expected to survive, and the state athletic commission was itching to ban Eoj for life. Eoj's soon-to-be former manager asked him, "Not for nothing, but don't you feel any remorse for killing those guys?"

"Absolutely not," Eoj barked and said, "Let me tell you something man, that could have easily been me."

His manager said, "I find that hard to believe."

"Look, man, I have a higher calling than most guys, I love what I do so immensely that it's hard to explain it. Some guys fight for money, fame, or simply to satisfy their egos, but I have an insatiable need to vanquish any challenger in the worst way possible when they come after my way of life and happiness, which is one and the same. Look I've got to go but keep me in the loop ok?"

"No problem," his manager said, and then hung up the phone and went into the kitchen where Mr. Stone was already having breakfast.

"Good time to talk?" he asked Eoj.

"Sure, let's talk."

窗体顶端

窗体底端

"Eoj, I'll be frank, I want to help you build a world where you can continue to do what you love to do and not have to worry about outcomes or consequences, someplace you can live happy, your own private paradise if you will. I know that you're your own man and not looking for or need any handouts, and I see no greed or deceit in you and you are a man of your word, and I would be honored to partner with you to help you achieve your goals."

Eoj replied, "Remember that works both ways, sir."

"I hope you like to travel," Mr. Stone said.

Eoj replied, "I do."

Mr. Stone then raised his glass of OJ and Eoj did the same. "Here's to a long and prosperous partnership."

Eoj replied, "Amen to that."

Two days later, Eoj got the call that the big guy didn't make it and he had to come in to the state athletic commission. His former manager said he'd meet Eoj there. Eoj thanked him and then asked John to borrow a car for the trip to the city, and John asked him if he'd rather be flown in. Eoj declined and said that a drive would be good for him.

"Sure," John said, and told him to take any car in the garage he wanted, and if he needed any info on any of the cars, the houseman would be happy to help him.

John then handed Eoj a card key for a garage that would be nearby and keys to an apartment he owned, also close by, just in case he would run late and didn't want to make the drive back that night. "And Eoj," John said, "there's someone there 24/7 to look after your needs."

Eoj said, "I feel like I'm on my way to paradise right now."

John smiled and said, "Have a good trip," and Eoj thanked him and picked out an Aston Martin for his trip and headed out.

Eoj took one of the service roads to open up the car before getting to the main highway to see what kind of power the car had. He pushed down hard on the throttle and the car never hesitated to show Eoj what kind of power he was dealing with. "Whoa," Eoj said to himself, "no way this engine is stock." He would learn a lot more about these cars later on.

Once in the city, he meets up with his former manager and heads into the state athletic commission to deal with whatever decision they made about his career, and their decision was that Eoj would be banned for life. "There's simply no room for that kind of savagery in this sport," and with that, it was over for Eoj, at least in this world.

As he left the building, they ran into a crush of reporters and spectators, and they started shouting questions at the men. Eoj stopped and said a few statements only: "I have no remorse for those two men, for it was them who deceived themselves into thinking that they could take on a war by themselves. They were ill-advised and ill-equipped to do so and they paid for it. Now, would you nice people step aside and let us by."

The crowd went silent and let them pass. Eoj then bid his former manager goodbye and said that he would stay in touch.

Not in the mood to drive back to the country, he decided to explore the city for a bit before heading to the apartment for the night. When Eoj got to the apartment, he had to take a private elevator that went directly to the duplex. "Nice…very nice," he said to himself. Eoj was a man of few words.

A moment later, the intercom rang.

"Yes," Eoj answered.

"Good evening, sir," the voice on the other end said. "I'm Jane. If you should need anything please don't hesitate to ring me, and would you like breakfast, sir?"

"Why yes, thank you, Jane. Good night."

"Good night, sir."

When Eoj went to the kitchen the next morning, he was taken aback at the spread that Jane had laid out for him to enjoy.

"Good morning, Jane. Wow! Are we expecting company?"

"Just myself and one other staff member who's stopping in a little later."

"Oh, ok. Well please join me, I would love to have some company."

"Sure," Jane said, and they sat and enjoyed breakfast and each other's company.

After breakfast, Eoj thanked Jane. Jane replied, "Anytime," with a big smile on her face. "Be safe."

"Thanks, I will," Eoj replied as he headed out.

On his way back to the country, he thought to himself, *now that's how you start your day.* He was also thinking about his next order of business, avenging John Stone.

Once back in the country, he sat down with John and told him that he wants to take care of that clown before moving forward with plan B. "Only one problem," Eoj said, "he knows me."

"That's not a problem," John said. "We'll just appeal to his weaknesses, cash and pride, but Eoj, you can't kill this guy, just give him something to remember you by."

"No doubt," Eoj replied.

John Stone rented a private gym in an undisclosed location for a weekend, and the pro who did a number on John would not know the exact location until one hour before the fight. John was able to entice the pro into a two-round fight with Eoj for 50k cash, half now and the other half when he shows up.

Eoj had met up with the pro to deliver the first half of the money, and as he handed him the money, Eoj said to him, "Don't make me come looking for you on fight day."

The pro snapped back at Eoj, "Who the fk you think you talking to? You just make sure you be there and you better have my money b*h." He then laughed and walked away, and Eoj thought to himself, *I like this guy, he's got a few screws loose, this is going to be so much fun.*

Eoj then thought about a rule of engagement of letting people be themselves and do whatever they needed to do to prep for a fight with him.

It's fight day and Eoj and John arrive to the gym early so they can meet these guys as they came through the door. Mr. Stone had also arranged to have one of his small but elite security teams to be there to make sure things wouldn't get out of hand.

Once there, Mr. Stone informed the pro and his crew that as a good-faith gesture he would like he and his crew to be searched for any weapons, phones, or recording devices before they entered the gym, citing that anything that happens in this gym today stays in this gym.

"Your property will be returned."

"No problem," said the pro.

After being searched, security turned up guns and phones. Mr. Stone and Eoj just looked at the men and said nothing about the find, and then informed the pro that the fight would start in a half an hour promptly, and then Mr. Stone handed him the other half of the money.

It's fight time and both men are in the ring, waiting for the bell to sound. The pro has two cornermen and Eoj has no one in his corner.

The pro has a cocky kind of confidence, talking smack and making gestures at both John and Eoj. John ignores him, but Eoj responds with his blank killer-white stare. Just then, the bell sounded for the start of the first round. Both men met at center ring. The pro threw a couple of combos at Eoj and couldn't understand how he missed, so he started trying to avoid Eoj by backpedalling and staying to the outside of the ring, and he was pretty fast at running away. Eoj just let him with a sinister grin on his face.

The bell sounded to end the first round. The pro looked surprised and started to smile, and then told the guys in his corner that this was going to be the easiest 50k he ever made.

Just as the bell sounded for the second round, Eoj looked at John and winked at him. The pro started to back away and in an instant, Eoj had cut off the ring and landed a blistering right to the jaw. It was broken. The pro got up slowly and Eoj then said to him, "You're gonna have to go off your meds to keep up with my madness," and then Eoj ripped into him with a vicious onslaught of body and head shots and deadly combos.

The gym went silent. It was the first time those guys had seen violence like that with such precision. They all stood in awe as Eoj got out of the ring, leaving the pro on the canvas, a broken man. He then informed them that there was an ambulance outside waiting for their friend. Eoj and John then left the gym.

The men then carried the pro out to the ambulance, collecting their things as they left and still looking confused and in disbelief that this whole event was premeditated.

Later that evening, Eoj and John met up at one of New York's finest steakhouses. At the table, John thanked Eoj for his gift and dinner and Eoj replied, "Don't forget to have dessert."

John said, "Indeed," and both raised their drinks and toast to it.

Eoj then said to John, "Let's discuss the rules of engagement for plan B."

"Sure, what did you have in mind?"

"I think the only rule should be that they should know that only using their hands is allowed and anything else would be met with fierce enforcement and a body bag, period. Doping is encouraged and going off your meds is welcomed. You may prepare in any way you wish before meeting and engaging in war with your most gracious host, the ALPHA of your OMEGA … the MARKSMAN!!!"

John then tells Eoj, "We're gonna have to make you a title belt worthy of your talents and build a house arena on one of the properties for the domestic fights."

Eoj replies, "No doubt."

John then said to Eoj, "Hey, why don't you take some time off while we get this done and set your inaugural fight? You have everything you need and if you don't, it's just a call away, go enjoy yourself and I'll see you when you get back."

Eoj then went to his room to make plans.

Suddenly, a grin came across Eoj's face. He was thinking about a couple of places he was going to go, Vegas was one of them and his childhood neighborhood was the other. Vegas was a blast, Eoj met some interesting people and did some interesting things, including winning big at the black jack table, he thought to himself not bad for a first timer.

But all the old hood seemed to do was refresh his rage and madness and he found himself lusting for battle, it was time to go home.

Once back, John Stone greeted Eoj and then informed him that he had something for him. They went into the living room and made themselves drinks. John then motioned for Eoj to a big table with a large cloth on it, but what Eoj didn't see is what was under the cloth.

John asked Eoj, "Are you ready to start your journey?"

"Absolutely," Eoj replied.

Then John pulled the cloth to reveal Eoj's championship belt. Eoj was taken aback by this stunning work of art. John describes it to Eoj as one of one, it will never be duplicated.

Made of the finest platinum, 24k gold, silver, diamonds and other precious gemstones and 4 inscriptions, all in diamonds, and they read as follows from top to bottom. 1st. Supreme 2nd. Excelsior 3rd. Alpha of your Omega. 4th. And on the rear strap, One Of One.

It has six interchangeable belts made of the finest leathers with lamb skin lining in Eoj's favorite colors; black, tan, red, white, blue, and green. And the cost of this belt John revealed was a well spent ten million dollars.

Eoj then asked John when his first fight would be. "In a couple of weeks."

"Can't wait," Eoj replied.

Eoj never really needed to train at the gym, his talents were supernatural, he was simply meant to do this. The only form of training for him was running and he loved it, running 5 to 10 miles a day on the norm.

Eoj's first fight would be a home fight and he and John would be hosting the challenger and his team for a week until fight night. These fighters were sponsored by very wealthy individuals from all over the world and locally, who were very fond of watching such a barbaric and violent sport which sometimes ended in death for the weaker man.

Millions were made and lost every fight. Eoj would be the only fighter with a ten million belt on the line every time he fought as a bonus, the other sponsors would put up other things like luxury cars, condos, seasonal sports tickets, etc. These bonuses kept the fights very interesting and the spectators on the edge of their seats.

The 300 seat arena John built rivaled the pro arenas and had every amenity one would need. The ring would be dressed in one of Eoj's favorite colors on any given day. The ring had Eoj's ring name and logo dead centered, THE MARKSMAN and a pair of gloves hanging from a nail and dripping blood and leaving a puddle of it.

It's fight night, and Eoj is in his locker room having a pair of custom made 8 oz gloves laced on, any of the fighters could wear the same, in fact, they don't have to wear gloves at all as long as they use their hands only during the fight as stated in the rules.

On his way to the ring, the crowd is cheering loudly to the song "Another One Bites the Dust" by Queen. Any fighter can request theme music for their ring entry. Eoj would simply listen to what's already playing or request nothing at all.

Once he got to the ring, Eoj got a good look at his opponent, the guy was a 320 lb behemoth and former power lifter nicknamed Silverback from Congo Africa. This guy dwarfed Eoj; Eoj was a chiseled 215 pounder. Eoj was considered a small heavy weight by today's standards and this is what made him so unassuming, possessing such deadly power and speed, not to mention the rest of his raw talents and hunger for destruction.

Eoj wanted to test the big guy's stamina and, if he didn't have any, take him out for a long swim and then drown his ass. The ring is decked out in red and gold, Eoj's code colors for when he's feeling dangerously wicked. John Stone is the only other person who knows the color codes and what they mean. As the men are waiting for the bell to sound, one can't help but feel the excitement in the air; it's contagious.

The bell sounds to start the first round and Eoj is already waiting center ring, waiting for the big guy to get there. Once he gets there, he tries to grab Eoj, but he side steps the big guy and launches a missile of a body shot that stops the big guy in his tracks. He then lets out a loud grunt and a toxic fart that momentarily makes Eoj lose focus and the crowd gasp. Silverback is now enraged and charges, and Eoj plants himself and lands a brilliant one-two to the nose. It's broken and blood is everywhere, and the ref takes a good bit of time checking out the big guy and finally gives the "ok" for the fight to continue. Just as Eoj was about to launch another assault, the big guy is saved by the bell.

Back in their corners, Silverback's people looked very concerned, and in Eoj's corner there was no one there, not even a stool, just the way he likes it. He says it keeps him focused on the business at hand.

Eoj never gets the 411 on his opponent before a fight because he loves the challenge of seeing how fast he can figure them out before taking them out, and right now he figured that Silverback is only good for a couple more rounds before he put his lights out.

The bell sounds for round two and the men meet center ring, and without hesitation Eoj launches a body assault on the big guy, peppering tremendous shots to the body. The big guy can't stand the sting of the 8 ozs and found himself on defense the rest of the round, something he never had to do before. And while sitting on his stool waiting for the second round to start, it was almost identical to the first, and he quickly realizes that the only thing he can do is try and fend off Eoj's vicious assaults because he was landing three to four shots to every one of Silverback's. The bell sounds to end the second round. Eoj leans over and whispers in the big guy's ear, "speed kills."

While sitting on his stool, he stares at Eoj in disbelief that someone so unassuming-looking is putting such a physical and unbearable beating on him. Silverback's anger and pride had gotten the best of him and he decided to throw dignity and respect out the window.

When the bell sounded, Silverback charged Eoj's corner, catching him slightly off guard. Eoj was able to side step the direct hit, but Silverback stuck his foot out in the process, tripping Eoj. Being aware of the rules, Silverback's team threw in the towel as a sign of surrender and pleaded with Eoj for mercy as well. And Eoj said nothing as he slowly approached Silverback with rage and death in his eyes. Silverback motioned to Eoj to bring it, and did he ever. The big guy stood straight up to face Eoj as he released his arsenal of destruction, including two kill shots. As the big guy fell to his knees and then his face, Silverback let out his last breath and died.

The arena went silent as two guys brought in Eoj's belt and placed it around his waist, and after seeing such a belt for the first time the arena broke out in loud cheers and whistles.

As Eoj left the ring, you could hear some people referring to him as the gorilla killer and the Phenom. Later that night, Eoj was back at John's estate, relaxing and admiring himself in the mirror with his belt on, and Eoj thought to himself, Man, what a belt and what a night, I must be dreaming, I feel so alive and empowered.

John got in a lil while later. He and Eoj spoke about the fight. John asked him, "How you feeling, champ?"

"I feel great, man, just great."

"You know, I thought you stick around for a while after the fight."

"Sorry, I don't really like crowds, but if you ever need me to just say the word."

"Thanks," John said. John then said, "Well, to the victor goes the spoils," and then motioned for Eoj to follow to the large living room, and sitting on the large table was a suitcase loaded with cash to the tune of 2.5 million and the bonus envelope with 50k cash.

John then said, "Here you are, sir, your take, spend it in good health," and Eoj quickly said, "what about the bonuses?"

John replied, "Those are strictly for you."

"OK, cool," Eoj said.

John then asked Eoj, "When do you think you would want to fight again?"

"Well, I think twice a month is more my speed."

John smiled and said, "Perfect, I was hoping you would say something like that."

John and Eoj then had drinks and dinner to celebrate. Eoj then informed John that he would be gone for a few days as he waits for John to set up the next fight, and John said, "Eoj, my toys are your toys, you only have to call and set up what you need. Have a great time, see you when you get back."

Eoj decided to stay local rather than a vacation; he needed to do something to release some rage he was feeling towards his father. He found that his contact info was still accurate and decided to give him a call. His father sounded surprised and nervous but invited Eoj over for a Sunday's dinner. Eoj said, "Good, I'll see you then," then hung up the phone and went through his files to find his dvd of his recent fight.

Eoj had decided on taking the Rolls Royce he nicknamed the car rage release. Driving was therapy for Eoj, and the Rolls kept him calm and happy. Sunday came, and while driving to his father's house, he found himself fighting flashbacks of his childhood, none of it good. Eoj harbored a fierce and furious anger towards his father, who is the main reason Eoj is the man he is today.

Suddenly he thought the visit may be a bad idea because he was already livid, but decided to follow through.

Once there, he drove up the driveway. A moment later his father appeared at the gate in front of the driveway to let Eoj know that they were doing a barbecue in the back yard. Eoj nodded his head and followed his father into the back yard and, with a half a smile, greeted his father's wife with a handshake; she seemed disappointed.

Before they could sit at the table, his father started asking him about the car and how much it cost, etc. Eoj abruptly interrupted his father and said, "I'm not here to talk about the car."

His father then nodded his head and said, "Ok."

They all sat and had dinner with some small talk about the weather, work, etc. Once dinner was over, Eoj asked his father to speak with him in private. "Sure," he said and led him into the living room.

Eoj then asked his father to have a seat; he did, and Eoj then pulled a dvd out of his inside jacket pocket and turned on his father's tv and player and played the dvd. His father nervously smiled and asked, "What is this?"

Eoj said, "It's a thank you," and his father said, "Oh ok," and turned his attention back to the tv to watch the dvd. It was Eoj's first pro fight. He had his face blurred out until the end of the fight, and before revealing himself, he asked his father what he thought of the fighter who won the fight.

"Well, I've never seen anything like that in my life. That guy's an animal, a straight up killer, an assassin in boxing gloves. No pro can handle that guy."

"That's right," Eoj said, and then revealed his face, and his father was shocked and speechless. Eoj continued, "I'm not a pro, I'm something far better … and worse, thanks to my parents. So thanks for the abuse, hatred, deadly beatings, and neglect. It really made me the man I am today. I never want to ever see your face ever again unless you die and I get to bury you and send your ass straight to hell." And with that, Eoj took his dvd and left his father standing there stunned.

On his way home, he encountered a traffic jam, and after sitting in slow traffic for ten minutes, he saw the root of the problem. It was a broken down car, and it seemed no one wanted to stop to help the young lady in distress. Eoj couldn't believe what he was seeing: such a pretty young woman that no one seemed to want to help.

As he got closer, he could see that she was crying. Eoj pulled over in front of her car, then got out and walked over to where she was and asked her if she was ok and asked how he could help.

When she looked up to Eoj, he was shocked by her beauty. She then said to him that her engine light had come on, the car made some loud noise and died, but she was able to pull over safely, but had no luck getting help because no one would stop and her phone was dead.

Eoj offered his phone and asked her where she was headed, and she told him, "The city." After using Eoj's phone, she could still get no help.

Eoj offered to have her car towed to wherever she needed it to be and drop her to where she was going also. She smiled and agreed and thanked Eoj, and they walked to the car. When they got in the car, Eoj made a call and made arrangements to have her car towed to her mechanic's shop. Once done with the call, Eoj noticed her checking out the car. "Wow," she said, "This is some fancy car you got here."

"Um," Eoj said, and then stuck his hand out and said, "I'm Eoj."

She said, "Nice to meet you, I'm Michelle."

Eoj noticed that his anger had subsided while with Michelle, and it brought a rare smile to his face.

After getting Michelle to her destination, Eoj asked her for her contact info, and she said, "Sure," and handed him her business card and said, "You can call me anytime."

Eoj smiled and said, "I'm going to have to take you up on your offer."

"Please do," Michelle replied, and they bid each other goodnight. Eoj stayed in the city for the night in a great mood.

In the morning, he called John Stone to get his fight info, and John told him it would be in a week and that it would be another house fight. Before hanging up the phone, John asked Eoj, "Was everything ok?"

Eoj replied, "No doubt, I'll see you a couple days before the fight."

John said, "Ok, I'll see you then."

Eoj decided to give Michelle a call. She sounded happy to hear from him as they spoke on the phone. Eoj then asked her when could he see her again, and she let out a soft sigh and said, "Any time this week would be fine," because she had some time off.

Eoj was delighted to hear this and set the date for Friday night, the night before his fight. He figured if she was having a good time that maybe she would stay a couple of days with him.

When Michelle heard where she was going, she informed Eoj that she was a little nervous about driving so far and wouldn't be looking forward to driving back to the city late night by herself. Eoj then let her know he figured as much and he had transportation in place for her and he would be picking her up and taking her home, and to that she replied, "Well, I'm good then. I'll see you Friday."

"Absolutely," Eoj replied, and they ended the call.

Eoj then gave John a call, let him know his plans and that he would be using the guest house for the weekend and that there was someone he wanted John to meet. John sounded excited and said he couldn't wait and to be safe.

Eoj replied, "No doubt, see you soon."

It's Friday, and Eoj just arrived at Michelle's apartment, and she's already in front waiting for him, and he is mesmerized by her presence. She's wearing blue jeans, and her hazel green eyes match her yellow top and sandy blonde hair perfectly. Eoj gets out to let her in, and their eyes lock on one another. Both are smiling broadly, and suddenly, Michelle gives Eoj a kiss on the cheek as she enters the car. Once Eoj enters the car, she tells him that the car looks more beautiful in the daylight. "Thanks, I agree," Eoj said.

"So are you ready for a great night?" Eoj asked.

Michelle replies, "Yes, please," and gives a smile, "How long of a drive do we have? I've never been this far out on the Island."

Eoj informs her that it's almost a two-hour drive if they were driving.

"You mean we aren't driving?"

"No," Eoj replies, "The chopper will get us there in 45 minutes. I hope you're not afraid of flying."

"Not in planes," Michelle said, "but this would be my first time in a chopper."

"First time for everything," Eoj chimed in and they both smiled.

Michelle then said, "You're just full of surprises aren't you?" Eoj replies, "Sometimes."

Once aboard, Michelle noticed it was decked out in roses and champagne.

"Very impressive," Michelle said.

"Thanks, what's your music preference?" and she says old school R&B. "Likewise," Eoj said and put the music on.

As they were served the champagne and strawberries, Eoj and Michelle toasted to a great night and new beginnings. Once they arrived at the

Estate, there was a golf cart waiting for them at the landing pad. Eoj drove to the main house and showed Michelle the guest house along the way. She was very impressed and asked, "Is this where you live?"

"Sometimes, and also in the city and also at my apartment in queens," Eoj explained, "I travel a lot so they come in handy."

Michelle said, "I hope you don't travel too much," and gave a big smile.

"Not too much," he smiled back.

At the main house, Eoj told Michelle, "I want you to meet a very good friend of mine," while introducing her to John Stone.

"Nice to meet you," Michelle said.

"Pleasure," John replied.

Then they all went inside to get better acquainted. At the dining table they shared small talk about current events, the weather, etc.

After dinner, John told Michelle to enjoy her stay and was looking forward to seeing her again.

"Why, thank you, likewise," she said.

"Eoj," he said, "See you at the fight."

"No doubt," Eoj replied, and the men bid one another good night.

Michelle seemed puzzled and asked Eoj, "Are we going to a fight?"

Eoj explained to her, "Well, I have to go but you don't if you're not into that sort of thing, I'd definitely understand."

Michelle said, "No, I like watching fights, who's fighting?"

"I am," Eoj replied.

Michelle said in a low voice, "You are?"

"Yes," Eoj said, "Let's go to the house and we can talk about it there if you like."

"Sure," she said and they went to the guest house. Eoj decided to be totally honest no matter the consequences.

As they sat in the living room Eoj cautioned Michelle that his story was a long one and still may not cover everything and that they should at least have some dessert.

"I'd love some dessert," Michelle replied.

Michelle had her favorite, carrot cake, and Eoj had an ice cream sundae with the works. When Michelle saw it she said, "Wow, I'm jealous, will that interfere with your fight tomorrow?"

"Not at all," Eoj responded, "It'll be as if I never had it, besides, I'll burn that off on my 10k run in the morning."

Michelle asked, "The morning of your fight?"

"Yes, but it's the norm for me. I know most fighters rest up on there fight day, but everyone is different. You see, Michelle, coincidently I'm entering two new worlds at once, a world I wish to build with you, and a world that's on the dark side of fighting, you see, I'm not a professional, I'm something far better and far worse, I'm not saying this to scare you in any way, I'm just being honest, babe, because I never lie and would expect the same from you."

Michelle smiled and said, "Of course."

"At a early age, I've had this knack for fighting and lost a lot of friends and even potential girlfriends and it was because they didn't know how to respond to me after watching me absolutely annihilate another person the way that I did. Most were to afraid to approach or speak to me and those who did speak would say very little, but all agreed that what they witnessed was something supernatural and violent beyond belief."

Michelle had a concern look on her face and then asked Eoj if he ever hurt anyone he loved. "Never," Eoj replied, "that I'm only violent when I'm defending myself, someone I love, or my property, otherwise, I'm one of the nicest guys you'll ever meet. I give you my word and my word is steel solid."

Michelle gave a beaming smile and Eoj knew she understood him.

They touched on many subjects as the night slowly went by. Some of the subjects were childhood, past relationships, work, and the near future. Upon their talks Eoj found that Michelle and her family were devout Christians and she was VP of her father's nonprofit charities. And Michelle asked of Eoj and John's relationship and partnership. It was the break of dawn and they had talked through the night, and Eoj told Michelle he had to do his road work and he would be back in time for breakfast if she was up for it, and she said she was looking forward to it. She then gave Eoj a kiss on the cheek, they both smiled at one another and Eoj was off to do his road work.

Eoj does a five minute mile so he was back at the house within the hour. After breakfast, Eoj and Michelle spoke about their plans for the day. Eoj was just going to relax and take a nap later to be ready for the fight and then told Michelle that he'd understand if didn't want to stay and would see to it that she gets home safely.

"No," she replied, "I want to be here for you always," she was already falling for Eoj and he for her.

Eoj then gave a smile and thanked her. He then called the staff at the arena and ordered that the ring be dressed in green and gold, which meant he was in a good and more than likely not going to kill his opponent tonight. When John saw the ring that night, he smiled and said to himself good choice for a first impression.

Meanwhile, it's just about that time and Michelle is with him in his locker room and Eoj tells her, "Remember, my lady, it can get really ugly out there and at any time you feel that you feel uncomfortable, there's an escort standing by to take you back to the house and I will join afterwards."

Michelle replies in a soft voice, "Ok. baby."

Eoj then tells her she looks stunning and thanked her for being there for him and they kissed and she was escorted to her seat.

Once at her seat Michelle thought to herself, what a spectacle this place was, first class all the way, luxury floor boxes with a personal attendant to see to your needs.

Michelle looks up at the ring and sees Eoj's opponent already there waiting on him, grooving to his theme music. Suddenly the lights go dim for a few seconds and when they come back on, Eoj is also standing in the ring in all his glory for all to see, and no one can seem to take their eyes off it, his ten million dollar belt. Michelle couldn't wait to see that up close and personal after thinking to herself, *oh my god what is that thing?*

After walking around the ring to give everyone a good look, two men from Eoj's security team relieved Eoj of his belt. Eoj's opponent is a 6'2, 250 lb rough fighter from Cuba nicknamed the Cuban demon who's notorious for breaking rules.

The men are in their corners waiting for the bell to sound. As soon as the bell sounds, demon rushes Eoj and gets drop with a thunderous right hook. He then tries to grab Eoj on his way down to the canvas and receives a second bomb to head that puts him flat on his face. As Eoj is directed to the neutral corner the demon grabs his leg, an annoyed Eoj quickly pulls his leg free.

While waiting for the eight count to be over Eoj decided to dismantle the demon's body. The ref gave the signal to continue the fight and the demon started to back step and Eoj rushed him and landed a deadly combo. Body, body, head and dropped the demon once again, but this time it cost him his mouth piece and a couple of teeth and he was starting to bleed pretty badly. After barely bringing himself to his feet, he was saved by the bell.

While the men were in their corners, Michelle noticed that Eoj was standing alone in his corner looking as calm as can be and haven't broken a sweat yet. And in the demon's corner there was cause for concern, they were having a hard time stopping the bleeding and wanted to throw in the towel, meanwhile Eoj was just warming up.

The bell sounds to start round two and the demon is already looking like he's been through a war and a half. As the demon slowly makes his way to the center of the ring, Eoj senses a plead for mercy coming from the demon, not his forte, and decides it's time to put him down.

Eoj puts on his sinister snarling face and unleashes an unrelenting barrage of body breaking shots that would be ruled cruel and unusual punishment in a lesser arena, but not here where that kind of savagery is expected and encouraged.

The Cuban demon is done and goes down hard, hitting the canvas directly in front of Michelle's seat where she cringes and drops her drink. The crowd goes crazy with cheers and whistles, and the security team wraps Eoj's belt around his waist and he then raises his hands beaming with pride. He and Michelle make eye contact and then smile at each other. Eoj then motions for her to meet him back at the locker room, she nodded and headed out with the security team. On her way out, Michelle noticed the diverse group of people dressed in their red carpet best, both the men and women.

Also the Cuban demon being taken out on a stretcher through a different exit. Once back in the locker room, Michelle ran over to Eoj and gave him a long and hard embrace and asked him if he was ok.

Eoj said, "I'm fine, baby, how about you?"

"I'm good, baby, hey, I hardly recognized you when you're handling your business."

Eoj then pulled her closer and said, "Just remember, babe, when I'm taking care of business, I'm all about the business and my business never interferes with my pleasure," Michelle then smiled and said,

"I like that." Just then, John came over to greet them and asked Eoj if he would have time to greet some guest before he and Michelle leave to be to themselves.

"Sure," Eoj said, "and let's do the feedback booth at breakfastm,"

"Sounds good," John replied.

After greeting some people that John wanted him to meet, Eoj and Michelle went back to the guest house for a celebratory dinner. At the table Eoj said to her, "I know you have some questions, so ask away."

An excited and curious Michelle then asked, "May I see that belt of yours and what exactly is the feedback booth? I mean, I think I know what it means just by the name, Eoj."

"Not to worry, I'd be happy to explain it to you. First, the feedback booth is a very sophisticated piece of equipment that we use on every fighter before and after a fight and get full 3D body scan and health report that tells us if a fighter is healthy enough to fight and what kind of damage was done after a fight in detail, it's a life saver for those who may have a life threating condition they may not be aware of. Everyone must go through the booth before and after, because we do not accept reports from anyone else, period, it's the best way to keep the playing field levelled here at least. And ah yes, the belt, let's see it should be around here somewhere," he said with a big grin on his face and said, "come with me my lady."

Michelle followed Eoj to the living room to a huge display cabinet and there it was, lighting up the whole room. Michelle was in awe of this stunning piece of art made of precious metals and stones and the inscriptions brought a more serious look to her face.

Eoj asked her, "What's wrong?"

Michelle said that after looking the belt over that she now realized what she just witnessed out there, "it was like the belt described you in perfect detail," she said, "I've never seen or heard of any boxer with such capabilities and oh my god," she said, "may I ask—"

And Eoj interrupted her and said, "You may, it cost ten million dollars, babe."

Michelle gasped and said, "oh my goodness."

Eoj then asked if she would like to try it on for size.

"Really," she said, and before she could answer, Eoj wrapped the belt around her waist and said, "her you are champ."

Michelle stumbled as she tried to stand up straight, and then said, "Whoa, how much does thing weigh?"

Eoj replied, "hum, I'm not sure, somewhere between 15 and 20 lbs. It's one of one hence the inscription on the rear," Eoj said.

"That's for sure," Michelle replied.

"Let's have some dinner," Eoj said, "I'm famished."

The next morning they met John at the main house for breakfast to go over upcoming events and the feedback report.

At the table, everyone greeted one another and then got right down to the business at hand. John showed Eoj the two dates for his next fights and Eoj looked at them and said, "That works,"

John replied, "Very good, oh" he said, "Here's the feedback report," Michelle then turned her attention to John as he started to read it.

"Well," he said, "Let's see, this was his very first defeat as he suffered a broken jaw, a fractured cheekbone, some broken and bruised ribs and a concussion, Damn Eoj this reads like a grocery list," Eoj replied thanks. "By the way, your take is back at the guest house, also how's your calendar besides the fight dates?" John then asked.

"Well, I'm going to take a week and take this young lady to paradise and then I'll be local till the fight."

"Very good, enjoy your time and I'll see you see you when you get back."

Eoj replied, "No doubt," as they left the main house.

On their way back to the guest house, Michelle, with a big smile on her face, asked Eoj, "Hey, where is paradise?"

He smiled back at her and said, "Sorry, I meant to ask you if you had any time off to go first."

"Don't worry, I always have time to go to paradise," she then paused and then said, "-with you, babe."

A couple of days later they were on their way to Hawaii. Once on the jet, Michelle told Eoj, "I can get used to this."

"And so you should," Eoj said.

Once in their suite, Michelle expressed a need for a heart to heart and sat Eoj down and asked him what was wrong, and before he could answer, she said, "I've been waiting for you to make a move baby, to no avail, is it me?"

Eoj had a sad look on his face and said, "Yes it is."

Michelle had a concerned look on her face as she braced herself to hear what he had to say, "Listen, baby," Eoj said, "I was never very good at getting my point across verbally and I'm sorry about that baby but I've been working on that. I've never had a relationship where I was afraid of losing, and with you, I'm terrified of losing, Michelle, when I first met you I just knew I was in the wrong place, because how could I be so lucky to make your acquaintance with my wicked ways. I knew right away that you were special and your love sacred, I knew that I had to be in the right place and time before expressing myself to you, sweetheart."

Michelle smiled with tears streaming down her face and said, "That was beautiful baby and I do believe we were in the right place and time, so now, tell me what you need to say so we can make this a great time baby."

Ok sweetheart, here goes, Michelle, I um, I um…want to ravage your body with a savage kinda loving," Michelle had a shocked look and a nervous smile on her face and Eoj quickly interjected and said, "Damn, that didn't come out right,"

Michelle said, "That's alright, baby, I know what you meant," and they both smiled and Michelle then said, "I really felt the intensity of that bold statement of yours and to be honest, it got me kinda hot," Michelle then whispered, "Now come over here and take me to paradise."

Morning came and Eoj awoke to a smiling Michelle and she then said to him, "I'd really like to see that place one more time before we get up for breakfast,"

Eoj smiled and said, "No doubt," and they stayed in bed a while longer.

Soon, it was time for breakfast and Michelle was getting out of bed and leaned towards Eoj, she then whispered in his ear, "your love is king."

Her words left him speechless and he embraced and kissed her and then said, "Thank you, sweetheart."

Once back from paradise, they stayed local being that the fight was only a couple of weeks away, but something strange was happening with Eoj.

Michelle noticed it first when they were at dinner one night, things were going fine until he put his head in his hands and started grimacing as if in pain, a concerned Michelle then asked, "Sweetheart, are you ok?"

Eoj said, "I'm not sure, babe, but I think I need to get home." "Sure, sweetheart, I'll drive," being that they were in the city and only across town from the apartment, that's where they went. Once there Eoj told Michelle that he had to go out and would be back soon, Michelle didn't question him and said that she would be there when he got back, Eoj then gave John a call with a rather strange request, John obliged him and told he would meet him at the private gym within an hour.

When Eoj showed he was happy to see John and the five sparring partners he requested and his special 8s. John gave Eoj a concerned look and Eoj told him not to worry and that he was only going to bruise their egos." Eoj went through 4 of the men like hors d'oeuvres before the main course hors d'oeuvres before the fifth man turned down his 10k and quit.

After the episode, the men left on their own power, Eoj and John then left leaving the security team to shut everything down. John then asked Eoj if he was ok, "I am now," Eoj replied. "You never cease to amaze me, Sir, thanks for the treat."

"We'll keep some guys on retainer from now on."

"Thanks," said Eoj and went back to the apartment and John took the copter back to the estate. When he got back, Michelle rushed and embraced him hard and asked, "Was everything alright?"

Eoj said, "Yes, baby," and noticed she was crying. "Hey, there's no need for tears, sweetheart, everything's fine. I'm sorry I left you here by yourself, I know that had to be strange for you, it'll never happen again I promise."

Michelle wiped her tears and said, "It's not that, I thought that maybe I've done something wrong."

"On the contrary," Eoj said, "you've done everything right. Thank you for your love, sweetheart." Eoj then said to her, "Baby, sometimes my honesty is just as brutal as some of my fights," he then explained to her that he sometimes relieves his rage and happiness the same way. Eoj then sat Michelle down to try and explain things to her. "Listen baby," he said, "I've tried for years to purge this violent blood lust from the depths of my soul, tonight I was merely expressing my happiness since you came into my life and I know with you by my side I will get past this."

Michelle then said, "We will get past this together, I love you, baby, and will always be here for you, always."

Eoj then embraced Michelle and said no doubt. The fight was only days away so they headed back to the estate the next day to try and relax before fight. Michelle had to take a business trip for her father and the charity and would miss the fight. Eoj found himself needing a few more sparring matching to keep his demons at bay, and he knew it was because he was already missing Michelle.

Michelle strangely felt the sudden need to call Eoj. Once she got him on the phone she told him to have a good fight and that she would be back as soon as she could to be with him. Eoj replied, "No doubt, I love you to baby see you soon." He then headed to the garage to get a car and head to a nearby private gym where he was to meet the sparring partners, but once he got to the garage, there was Mr. Stone sitting in his newest toy, a Ferrari Enzo, and Mr. Stone then asked Eoj if he needed a ride. And Eoj said, "Absolutely," and they headed out to the gym.

Once there, Eoj realized he forgot his special 8s and gym bag in the foyer and John told him not to worry because he picked them up on his way out. "Cool," Eoj said as walked towards the gym.

John then asked, "Eoj, you ok," and he replied, "Yeah, just need to calm down a little before the fight."

"Ok, then let's get it done," John said.

It was a short night in the gym for Eoj, no one was killed but everyone was in some state of disrepair. Once it was over, John realized that Eoj was in total control of being out of control. As they left, John asked Eoj if he wanted to drive the new toy, no doubt was the response and there was laughter as Eoj opened up the Enzo.

Back at the estate, Eoj had his favorite dessert waiting for him, the victory ice cream sundae with the works, and John was having his usual extra large slice of Brooklyn's famous strawberry cheese cake. The men sat at the kitchen table to discuss the near future. John started in saying to Eoj, "I see that things are changing for the better in your life and I'm very happy for you and Michelle."

"Thanks," said Eoj, "she's the genuine article and my best future."

John said, "I can tell you guys just click and you make a great couple. Hey listen Eoj, we came a long way and we both know this thing we have going isn't going to last forever and there's going to be a day where you and Michelle are going to need to have a life all your own."

"And I'm prepared for that time, Sir, so you won't have to explain anything."

"I only ask one thing of you when that time gets here."

"Anything," Eoj said.

John then said, "Let's go out like the 4th of July." "No doubt," Eoj said, "Consider it done."

John then said to Eoj, "Consider the belt a retirement gift so that one day your kids could see how great their father was at his craft, and our relationship and partnership everlasting."

Eoj then got up and walked over to the bar and made drinks for a toast. After giving John his drink they raised their glasses and toasted 'to everlasting', and then the men called it the night.

Back at the guest house, Eoj needed to hear from the love of his life and called her. It was almost 3am and a sleepy Michelle answered the phone in a soft voice, "Hello," she said, and when Eoj said 'hello, my love' she came to life saying, "Baby, I'm so glad you called."

Eoj then said, "Sorry for waking you but I had to hear your sweet voice before going to sleep baby."

Michelle then said, "Never be sorry, my king, I always want to hear from you, always. How's it going on your end?"

"Great," Eoj responded. "Hey, when will you be back?"

"I'm still scheduled for the night after your fight, baby."

"Ok, cool," Eoj said, "we'll talk before the fight love have a great night."

Michelle responded, "I will now, my king, good night."

The next morning, Eoj ordered the ring to be dressed in black and gold for the fight that night. Later in the day, John noticed the ring and said to himself, whoa, and then called the gym staff to make sure they got it right and they said that they did. John knew that black and gold meant that Eoj was in a dark place and that spelled death for any opponent.

It was a few hours before fight time and Eoj was on the phone with Michelle and she sounded sort of sad. When Eoj inquired, she said, "I'm just missing you my sunshine."

Eoj replied, "I can't wait to see you either, my queen, not to worry, we'll be in each other's arm's soon."

Michelle said, "Promise, I do baby I do. Eoj," she then said, "you make me so happy."

"Likewise, my love, see you soon," and with that he called the gym staff and had them change the ring to green and gold and ordered the jet be ready for flight after his fight, destination Florida to be with Michelle.

Just before fight time, John walked into the arena and noticed the ring change and smiled because taking on Eoj was hard enough but watching an ordered killing was really quite difficult to watch.

Fight time and Eoj's opponent is an Italian brute from Eoj's childhood borough of Brooklyn going by the ring name (Luna man) weighing in at 255 lbs. and 6'3 tall, he's juiced on the roids and loves pain, but Eoj won't find that out until he engages this brute. The feedback report before the fight showed that Luna has major frontal lobe damage and also extensive damage from a number of concussions which makes him extremely violent and dangerous.

On his way to the ring, Eoj hears Luna's theme music of choice, thunderous car crashes, train wrecks, and truck wrecks. Eoj thought to himself this should be good. Once in the ring, Eoj gets a good look at this guy whose body is covered in tattoos and scars and is crossed-eyed making him look like a demented cyclops.

While waiting for the bell to sound for round 1, the security team relieves Eoj of the belt and Luna starts taunting them as if he's going to take the belt from them, and then one team member tells Eoj on his way out, "This guy might really be nuts man."

Eoj replied, "We'll soon see about that."

The bell sounds and Luna just stands in his corner with a big grin on his face. Eoj said to himself ok, here comes your train wreck, my Cycloptic friend, and unleashed some tremendous body busting shots and face changing head shots that didn't seem to faze Luna as he went down to the canvas bleeding heavily from the mouth and face and still with that sinister grin on his face. As the ref came over to give the 8 count as Eoj was headed to the neutral corner, Luna jumped up, screamed and charged Eoj and caught him with a tremendously impressive body shot that temporarily stunned Eoj. It was the first time Eoj has gotten caught like that and the first time John Stone stood up out of his seat and looked concerned for Eoj. The bell sounded to end the first round. Eoj walked to his corner slowly and stood there by himself and John Stone was still standing waiting for a signal from Eoj to see if he was alright, and it came as Eoj motioned John to sit down. John then knew he was ok because he wouldn't lie about that.

The bell sounded for round two and Eoj ran across the ring and unleashed a gang of bad intentions on Luna, dropping him instantly, and he was just as quick to get up shouting, "Ok, let's go!" and babbling something in Italian repeatedly and kept coming after Eoj and getting dropped time and time again. Eoj thought to himself damn, this guy is on some wicked shit.

Finally, the brute started slowing down and Eoj started punishing him harder and slower and finally this bloody mess was over, there was so much blood everywhere, the canvas, all over Eoj and Luna, it was hard to tell if he was beaten or shot several times.

Eoj wanted to see the feedback info before he got on the jet, he wanted to know why this guy bled so much. On his way to the plane, John accompanied him to share the info with him, and it was disturbing, Luna had so many drugs in his system he should be dead John said, and the bleeding came from to many blood thinners, "you did manage to break his nose and a rib on either side and plenty of bruising internally and externally to go around." John then handed Eoj a small box with the key to a brand new Maserati in triple black. Eoj smiled and handed the key back to John and said, "Have fun breaking her in," and John smiled and said, "no doubt," and then they both laughed, John then told him that he would leave his take, "3 Million in the usual place in the guest house."

"Thanks," Eoj said, as they got to the plane Eoj said, "see you in a few days," John said see you when you get back.

During his flight, Eoj started thinking to himself, what the hell happened tonight and he knew John was thinking the same although he didn't say anything, Eoj kept asking himself what's different in his life, what would cause him to blink even for one second while in the ring and just like that he had his answer, his precious love, Michelle.

Eoj started to realize that he needed her rather than wanted her. Eoj was in love with Michelle deeper than the eternal abyss and was afraid to tell her because of previous experiences from past relationships, those women took his kindness for weakness and or just try to use him for what they could get from him.

Eoj never had a true love as Michelle and began to question why would a guy like himself be deserving of such a once-in-a-lifetime gift of true love.

He then picked up the direct line to the pilot to tell him to turn the plane around, but when the pilot answered, Eoj asked for the ETA (Expected Time of Arrival) instead.

He thought to himself, if there's anything in the world worth fighting it was true love, he then smiled to himself, reclined and asked the stewardess for a drink.

Once in Florida Eoj thought about picking up some Chinese food but then made a bee line straight to Michelle's hotel, he had the front desk ring her room so as to not scare her by knocking on her door directly, when they handed him the phone, it was still ringing, which brought a smile to his face because he got to her sexy sleepy voice, and she said hello in that soft sexy voice that drove Eoj crazy with excitement, Eoj answered saying, "special delivery for Michelle," and she squealed with excitement.

"Oh my god, honey, you're here! I love you! hurry up!" and hung up.

Michelle was waiting by the elevator when Eoj got to her floor, and when she saw him, she said, "Oh, baby," and took him by the hand and led him down the corridor to her room, leaning her head on his shoulder the duration of the walk.

Once in the room, she gave him a kiss and a great embrace and then lead him to the bedroom saying, "Come, my champion, paradise awaits us."

Morning came and Michelle had ordered breakfast and they enjoyed it in bed over small talk. As Eoj got up to take the trays away, Michelle saw the big black and blue bruise on Eoj's rib cage and gasp and said, "Oh my god baby what happened? Are you ok, baby?"

Eoj said, "Yes, I'm fine, just a little sore."

Michelle then asked, "did you make him pay for that, baby?" Eoj said, "no doubt, baby" and they shared a smile.

On their flight back, they had a heart felt heart to heart.

Eoj was talking about winding down his career and told her, "It may take 2 to 4 years but it will be done, baby," and that brought tears of joy to Michelle eye's and she then got out of her seat and knelt down beside his seat and placed her head in his lap and said, "Baby, if you need or want to take longer, I support you fully, my king," Eoj then took her by the hand and helped her up so she could sit in his lap for a while.

Eoj then told Michelle, "I think it's time to start thinking about a life of our own away from this lifestyle and build a future of our own, my love, what do you think?"

Michelle, with tears streaming down her face, smiled and said, "I couldn't agree more baby."

Eoj then said, "my love, I'm never going to hurt you ever and I'm—"

Michelle then interrupted him and said, "baby you don't have to say anything else, honey, our hearts speak to one another and our souls intertwine when we make love and when we are in each others company, its euphoric, now baby, if we're not a match made in heaven, it doesn't exist, baby,"

"I agree," said Eoj.

Back at the estate relaxing, Eoj asked Michelle "Hey, whatever happened to that old car of yours baby?"

She then said, "it's on its last legs, I'm going to have to replace it soon I guess, meanwhile I use mom or dads if I need to."

Eoj then took her by the hand and said, "let's take a walk," She smiled and said, "ok baby let's go."

They walked to the garage and Michelle said, "I thought you said a walk."

Eoj said, "we did, sweetheart, the walk is over, lets go get some dessert," and then opened the garage door to Michelle's delight.

"My god, honey, is this a garage or a dealership?" and Eoj said, "it sure could be, huh?" and they both laughed.

Michelle said, "they're all beautiful and I'm sure they all cost a pretty penny or two."

"That's true," Eoj said, "What say we go get that dessert?" and noticed that Michelle had her eyes on the Maserati he just won. He then gave her the key to it and said, "you drive," and Michelle let out a loud yeah sounding like a little girl for a moment.

On the road she was still grinning from ear to ear and then asked Eoj what he wanted for dessert and he said, "I already have an everlasting dessert." Michelle then looked at him curiously and Eoj then said, "you baby."

"Aww, honey, thanks me, too, I love you, but I still need my carrot cake tonight," and they both laugh.

Back at the guest house Eoj told her to drive to the back because he had a special spot to put her new car.

She said, "what did you just say baby?" and Eoj replied, "I have a special spot for your new car, baby."

Michelle then slammed on the breaks and said, "Ahh, honey, thank you so much, baby. How am I ever going to repay you?"

Eoj gave a grin and said, "I'm sure you'll think of something," Michelle then smiled and said, "I'm sure I will, you bad man."

Just as they sat down to enjoy their dessert, Eoj got a call from a brother he rarely speaks to so he knew it was bad news, and it was, his father only had days to live, if not hours.

He had a look on his face that Michelle had never seen before. She got nervous and said, "honey," Eoj didn't answer and she said a little louder, "baby please talk to me."

Eoj remembering his promise to Michelle then told her the news and said he was taking the copter to Queens to try to catch him before he passed. Michelle told Eoj, "I'm going with you," and Eoj said, "No, I'll be back late."

Michelle then said in a loud and firm voice, "Eoj I'm coming with you," he then looked at her, "of course you are, baby."

On their way there Michelle was holding his hand so tightly, Eoj gently placed his free hand on top of hers and whispered in her ear saying, "Honey, you've got to let the blood flow," while slowly spreading his fingers apart and mildly laughing to make light of the situation.

Michelle then looked at his hand and said, "Oh! Honey, I'm sorry I didn't realize, I'm so sorry."

Eoj said, "don't be, it's ok, baby, I see you've been working out, huh?"

"Just a little," she said. They shared a short laugh.

As they arrived, some of his family members were already in the waiting room crying and no one wanted to approach Eoj with the news that he was too late, but he could tell and looked at them and said in a loud voice, "what room?" and they told him. He then told Michelle, "please wait here, honey, I won't be long," and left for the room.

Michelle, not knowing what to do, started introducing herself and tried consoling them best she could.

Meanwhile, Eoj was in the room just staring at his father's body and then said in a low voice and a tear running down his cheek, "You wouldn't wait for me to get here so I could watch you suffer as you should, huh? you son of a bitch," and then he said in a loud thunderous voice, "YOU MOTHER*****," and it seemed the whole floor heard him as he came out of the room.

As he approached the waiting room all eyes were on Eoj as he reached out his hand for Michelle's. She took his hand, and on the way out Eoj said, "I'm going to call you," to his brother who called him.

Michelle was speechless in the copter as was Eoj. She could see tear tracks on his face and thought that he must have really loved his father deeply, but little did she know how wrong she would be. She went over to him and said to him, "honey, I'm so sorry you didn't get to say good bye to him and I know that kind of pain that can bring, baby."

Eoj interrupted her and said, "Hey, oh baby, I wasn't crying because he died, I was crying because I didn't get to see that mother***** suffer before he died."

Michelle was in shock, she's never heard such a profound statement before, even the stewardess started to cough and excused herself to the back of the chopper.

Michelle was in tears as the stewardess tried to comfort her. Michelle's tears turned to anger and she approached again saying, "Eoj, sweetheart, those are not the words and actions of a godly man."

Eoj responded, "baby, I don't even know what a godly man is or looks like," and Michelle realized he was serious and knew she had to help bring god into his life if they were to have a future.

She then told Eoj, "Ok honey, I think it's about time to learn who god is."

Eoj asked her if she knew who god was and if she believed in him and she said, "yes."

Eoj then said, "ok, I'm not a hard man when it comes to trying new things and if it makes you happy, baby, count me in because I never want to put tears in those beautiful eyes of yours unless they're tears of joy."

"Oh! Sweetheart, that's all I could ever ask of you."

He then apologized to the stewardess and gave Michelle a big embrace and said to her softly, "I love you and just want be happy together eternally."

Michelle said, "don't worry my love, we will be and you're going to love our god to."

Eoj replied, "if you say it then I believe it baby."

Back at the estate, John met them at the landing pad to greet them and offer his condolence. Eoj thanked him and said it was a hard shot but he's ok.

They all went to the main house where they had drinks and shared conversation. At one point John asked Michelle how she liked her recent gift and she said, "Oh my god! it's mind blowing and it's the second best gift ever gifted to me ever."

John and Eoj gave her a curious look and John then asked, "what was the first?" and Eoj chimed in, "and who gave it to you?" with a smile on his face.

Michelle then gently took Eoj by the hand and said, "Sweetheart, you are my first true and only true love gifted to me from god," and Eoj then said to Michelle, "Baby, you're my first and only true love also, I'm not worthy."

Michelle said, "You're more than worthy, my king."

John then said, "Ok, you two, do I have to leave the room?" and they all laughed.

Michelle then excused herself and bid John a goodnight and then walked over to Eoj and whispered in his ear saying, "Paradise is waiting for us, my king."

Eoj smiled and then said, "I won't be long, love."

He and John then talked business, they set the dates for next month's fights and Eoj let John know that he would be local until the fights, so he could meet and start getting to know Michelle's family.

John was pleasantly surprised because he knew where this was leading to and said, "that's great, enjoy your time, see you when you get back."

Eoj shot back, "no doubt," and went to join Michelle.

Back at the guest house he called his brother to let him know that he would be sending funds to take care of the arrangements and extra to put something in everyone's pockets.

Then he called out to Michelle and she answered, "In here baby," he knew her voice was coming from the bathroom and so he went in and there she was in a candle lit bubble bath and champagne on ice waiting to share.

"Wow," Eoj said.

"Join me?" Michelle asked.

"No doubt," Eoj said and Michelle giggled because she loved the way he says no doubt with such confidence.

While relaxing, they made the plans for Eoj to meet and start to get to know the family. They then toasted to a bright prosperous future.

The next morning Michelle called her parents to make dinner plans and her mom was happy to know that she was finally going to get to meet the man in her daughter's life and her father wanted to meet the man that makes his daughter so happy.

Eoj and Michelle drove to his apartment in Queens a few days before their planed dinner with her parents so they wouldn't have to take the long drive on the day of. Michelle liked the apartment saying that it was cozy and clean for a bachelor pad, "who did your cleaning, sweetheart?"

"Yours truly," Eoj said, "as a matter of fact I did all my cooking, cleaning, and laundry and still do when I have to."

"Wow," Michelle said, "I'm|Am I lucky or what."

"That's one thing mom taught me, besides, I was never the lazy type."

"Amen to that," she said and they both smiled.

"Hey, baby, what would you like for dinner tonight, we have just about anything nearby or we could go to the market and pick up somethings and I will cook up something really nice for us what do you say?"

"I say I'd love to have some of your cooking, baby, and I'll take care of dessert."

"No doubt!" Eoj said and Michelle giggled and they both smiled.

While at the market Eoj noticed a guy looking Michelle over and licking his lips and Eoj walked up beside him and the guy felt his presence then turned and faced Eoj, and Eoj said, "Man, that's some dangerous beauty isn't it?"

The guy smiled and said "it sure is."

Eoj then said, "you know she cost the last low life pervert who eyed her his miserable life," and the guy had the look of shock and fear on his face and before he could say anything, Eoj said, "hey man, ain't nobody got to hear you die, I'll just snatch your ass up and take you out that back door there and snap your f***ing neck like a twig," and with that the guy turned pale as a ghost and made a run for it. Eoj didn't give chase because he knew he would never see that guy again.

Michelle saw the commotion and asked, "What happened?"

Eoj said, "Oh! nothing that gentleman just thought he left his stove on."

"Oh," Michelle said, "Come honey I need your help with something."

"Ok, baby, no problem."

Back at the apartment Eoj made grilled salmon and baked potato and steamed green beans with garlic butter sauce. And Michelle made Eoj his favorite ice cream sundae with the works and she had her carrot cake and enjoyed a nice relaxing evening together.

The next morning at breakfast, Eoj gave Michelle a set of keys to the apartment and told her if she ever needed or wanted to use it she should never ask because what's his is hers," Michelle said, "Thank you baby, I can't believe how blessed I am and how things keeps getting better for us," Eoj said, "Things are only going to get better between us love. Hey, baby, tell me a little about your parents."

"Sure," Michelle said, "Well, they both are very involved in the church and our charity work and they are simple people and terribly honest and blunt to a fault."

"Ok, cool!" Eoj said.

The next day on their way to her parents for dinner Michelle said to Eoj, "You're not nervous are you, babe?"

"Just a little, I mean I don't want to say too much or too little you know what mean?"

"Yes, baby, I do. don't worry I'm there for you."

When they pulled up to the house, Michelle parents were sitting out on the deck relaxing and didn't take their eyes off of Michelle's new car until they got out, and as they did her mother said in a gleeful voice, "Michelle is that you baby?"

"Yes, mom."

Her dad then responded, "Whoa! what's that you're driving?" "It's a Maserati daddy." He then said, "Say, what?"

Michelle took Eoj by the hand and lead him over to her parents and made the introductions, "Mom and dad, this is the gentleman I've been telling you about, this is Eoj."

Eoj said, "nice to meet you, Ma'am, Sir," Her father then said, "Come on in, can I get you a drink?"

"Sure," Eoj said. The men sat in the living room while Michelle and her mother prepared to bring dinner to the table, meanwhile the men engaged in small talk.

"Dinner is served," the ladies called out and the men came to the table and pulled out the ladies chairs for them.

Both parents had questions for Eoj, first up was the mother and she asked in a low voice, "Eoj, dear, are you a model?"

He then smiled and said, "No, Ma'am but thanks for the compliment."

The father was next and said, "Eoj, I don't like to beat around the bush."

Just then Michelle gave her dad a look and said, "Dad don't."

Eoj chimed in and said, "honey, it's ok," and then said to her father, "Yes, sir," Her father then continued his question. "Let's talk near future, are you planning on making a honest woman out of Michelle and perhaps give us some grand children?"

Michelle said loudly, "Dad!"

"Sorry," he then said.

Eoj said, "Ouch, that was definitely blunt," Michelle couldn't help but smile and told Eoj, "Honey, you don't have to answer that baby."

Eoj said, "No, no, baby, I don't mind."

Her father then said, "See, he doesn't mind."

"Well, sir," Eoj said, "since Michelle is already a thief sir, I do plan on making a honest woman out of her in the near future."

Michelle's mother dropped her drink and her father started coughing out his food. Once he regained his composure all eyes were on Eoj and her father then asked, "Eoj, you care to explain that last comment?"

"Oh, sorry, sir, sure," he then explained, "you see, Sir, Ma'am your daughter here, stole my heart, so there's nothing else I can do or want to do but make an honest woman out of her in the near future."

The room went silent for a moment and then her father said, "Man, you are something else," and started laughing and her mother joined in saying, "Oh Eoj."

When he looked at Michelle she was smiling with tears in her eyes and then mouthed to him, "I love you baby," and he winked at her. And then they all enjoyed dinner.

The next morning, Michelle got a call from her mother and she told her how her father was still talking about Eoj's joke and that he liked him.

"I'm so glad to hear that mom," she said.

Her mother then said, "honey, I can tell there's something special about Eoj and your father felt it too as soon as he walked into the house, he has a presence that tells you everything is going to be alright while your with him, no harm will come to you, it's hard to explain honey but I can tell it's a positive thing, I'm not making any sense honey."

Michelle said, "Yes mom, I know exactly what you mean and your right and that's why I know he's my gift from god, everything is so right with us mom."

Mom then said, "Baby, you don't know how Iong I've waited to hear that."

Michelle then told her mother that Eoj was calling her.

"Ok," she said, "God bless you two, go be with him honey, we'll talk later."

"Yes, baby," Michelle said as she entered the living room, "Hey baby, come and tell me about the charities."

"Oh, ok," she said and sat beside him and explained how they would travel nationwide to provide god's love and what is needed by the poor, hungry, homeless, abused and the uneducated.

"Wow, baby that's huge, we do the best we can honey."

Eoj then said, "I'd like to be a part of that,"

"Well, you're welcome to come on board anytime babe, we can use all the help we can get."

"Cool," Eoj said.

Time was getting close to his first fight of the month and Eoj needed to talk to John about his finances.

Eoj needed a ride to the estate and Michelle was at work at the church so Eoj gave her a call to see what she was up to and explain his dilemma to her.

Michelle told him to feel free to take her mom's or dad's car if he was in a rush being that they were only 15 mins away, "or even better she said, "things are slow today and I don't need to really hang around today, baby," so if you would like some company I'd be more than happy to accompany you I could even spend the night if needed."

"I'd love nothing better, sweetheart," said Eoj, "See you in say 30 mins."

"Make it 20," Michelle said, and Eoj responded, "That's my girl," and hung up.

Michelle was there 20 mins later and tapped her horn a couple of times for Eoj and he came out and they were on their way.

"Wow," Eoj said, "You even got water and snacks, huh?"

"Nothing but the best for my king," she said.

"Well, thank you my queen."

Michelle then shut the engine and said, "Uh-oh."

"What's wrong?" Eoj asked.

"It's the engine."

"I think it's going to take a kiss to get it started again," Eoj looked at her and smiled and said, "you'll call me bad, huh?"

"I'm waiting," Michelle said.

Eoj then embraced her and gave her a big kiss and then said, "Let's roll."

"Now that's what I'm talking about," Michelle said and off they went.

At the estate, they went straight to the main house and greeted John and one of his lady friends.

Eoj thought to himself, John must be getting serious with her, he doesn't normally introduce his lady friends.

John then said, "Hey, why don't you ladies have a seat and maybe a drink while Eoj and I have a talk, we won't be long at all."

"Ok," the ladies said.

John and Eoj then went into John's office to talk and Eoj got right to it, asking how long it would take with all the investments that John has made on his behalf, what would be the time when he would be completely financially independent and have a self-sustaining entity.

John said, "With your properties and small businesses, I would say a minimum 2 years and then you would be good to go."

"Cool," said Eoj. "I can do that."

"I know you can, easily."

"Tell me something," John said. "I don't mean to pry, but you're emitting this sense of urgency."

Eoj then told John he found his purpose.

"Really?" John said excitedly and then asked, "What was it?"

Eoj told him about Michelle and the charities they run and said he thought, "this would the best way to leave a real mark on this world."

John's eyes widened and he said, "That's one of the best things I've heard from any of my friends or partners. Count me in Eoj, I'll match the donations dollar for dollar."

"John," Eoj said, "I know you to be a gracious and very generous man, friend, and partner. You know you don't have to do this for me at all, John, you've done more for me than you ever had to do and I'm forever indebted to you for that."

"Wow," John said, "Eoj, you've got to calm down and let me tell you what you've done for me. First, I don't know of anyone who can say they are close friends with the best fighter ever seen on this earth and who is practically immortal and can only be seen in action on the dark side of fighting."

"Eoj, it's because of you that I can entertain like no one else on my level, and you're the reason that my opponents, if you will, are willing to pay millions to watch their own hand picked monsters to take you on and you've shut every last one of those mother***ers down in the worst way possible."

"Eoj, watching you do what you do is like watching a god at play among mere men, so on the contrary, thank you. Now, please let me do this with you, I have more than I'll ever be able to spend in a hundred lifetimes and I'd be honored to help make the world a better place through the charities."

"Well, when you put it that way, I do," John said.

Eoj never thought of his dark talents that way before and took them for granted, he would just always wonder why the other guys could never faze him.

After their meeting, John and Eoj were feeling particularly hyped and decided to take the ladies and two of John's fastest cars to the nearby track to open them up. The Enzo and the lambo went screaming around the track sometimes at full throttle. The men were having a blast and the ladies were enjoying their wine and cheering them on.

On their way back to the estate Michelle said, "Wow sweetheart, where did you learn to drive like that, just watching you guys go down the track like that was exhilarating beyond belief."

"Well, maybe we should do this more often."

"Absolutely," Michelle said.

"Now, let's hurry back I want you to take me to paradise, baby."

"No doubt," Eoj said.

Michelle then giggled and said, "I love you."

"I love you too, sweetheart," Eoj replied.

Michelle then said, "Oh, by the way, I think John is getting serious with Lisa."

"You know, I thought the same being it was the first time he ever introduced one of his ladies friends."

"Oh, go John," Michelle said, "Yeah."

"Goodnight then, good for them," Eoj said.

"Right," Michelle said.

They stopped by the main house to say goodnight to John and Lisa before heading to the guest house for the night.

Back at the guest house, Michelle asked Eoj what caused he and John to be so excited.

"Oh, that was just a simple understanding we came to, and with that a great weight was simultaneously lifted off my shoulders and I can now see our future more clearly, baby, and it's as bright as the sun's might."

"Wow," Michelle said, "I love seeing you this way baby, I think all this excitement is catching on, now come over here my love and take me to paradise."

"No doubt," said Eoj and Michelle did her usual thing and they took the trip to paradise.

For the past year, things have been going according to plan for Eoj and Michelle. Eoj had been running through his opponents with the rage and destruction of a runaway freight train going one hundred miles an hour.

John had to continue to keep a stable of sparring partners on retainer to keep Eoj's fierce appetite for destruction satisfied. Michelle had to stop coming to the fights because Eoj was fighting at a fever pitch, taking on two opponents a month and endless sparring matches. It was simply too much for her to bear and she began to worry about Eoj's physical and mental well-being, although it didn't seem to faze him at all, and it didn't faze John either; he knew that Eoj was only reaching his pinnacle and had more than enough power left to finish their plans to go out like the 4th of July and retire his demons in a year, so he was just enjoying this phenomena because he knew Eoj was a once in a lifetime happening.

Eoj knew he needed to have a sit-down with Michelle about her concerns, so he called her and made dinner plans.

At dinner, he said to Michelle, "Hey love, I know what's on your mind, baby, I can see it on your face and feel it in your touch. I need you to know that you shouldn't worry about a thing. We are fine and even better, we're almost done with this thing."

Michelle said, "You're right, baby, it's just when I see both of your personalities more than I normally do in play, Mr. calm and that unhinged savage, it makes me a little nervous, baby."

"Not to worry, babe, you know I have them both in check."

"Ok, baby," Michelle said, "we don't need to go any further on this, let's just have a great night instead."

"Let's," Eoj responded.

"Mom and dad wanted to know, how did you like the service at church last Sunday?"

"Well," said Eoj, "I liked it, but I still don't understand why most of the people there still stare at us and John as soon as we come through the door."

"Well baby, ever since you and John started donating to our charities last year, we've been growing in leaps and bounds. At this rate, we may soon be able to go international as well. They think you guys are a couple down-to-earth celebrities and are starstruck whenever you guys show up. That's all it is, sweetheart."

"Oh, ok," Eoj said.

As time went by, Eoj spent more time with Michelle between fights, traveling on the charity's behalf, 'doing god's work' as Michelle likes to say.

Eoj even went back to his old neighborhood and opened two community rec/soup kitchens that are open year-round. He said it was one of his proudest moments.

Eoj said he also wants to open some self-help centers that would help people get their GEDs and prep them for job interviews. After getting back from their latest charity venture GED'S Eoj told Michelle that he needed some real excitement and Michelle said to him in a soft voice, "Sure, my love, but you'll have to let me take a nap first." Eoj then responded, "Baby, you're the best, but that's not exactly what I meant."

"Oh," she said, "what do you have in mind?"

"Las Vegas," Eoj said.

"Sin city?" Michelle asked.

"Yes, I've never been and don't worry, baby, you don't have to sin."

She laughed and said, "Ok, let's do it."

"Done," Eoj said.

"I'll see you after my nap, lover."

"No doubt," Eoj said and Michelle did her usual thing and then went into the bedroom to take her nap.

Eoj had an ulterior motive he left out, but was sure that Michelle wouldn't mind too much, being that he never gets to go see someone else fight, besides, this opportunity may never come again. You see, John had made arrangements for Eoj to meet the current undefeated heavy weight champion of the world and holding all four titles at once.

This guy's ego and arrogance and childish boasting had caught Eoj's attention and he felt the young man needed an attitude adjustment and wanted to invite him to his retirement event, so he could see the real world champion.

Once in Las Vegas, while passing by some of the casinoes, Michelle spotted one of the ads for the fight and she then asked, "Are we going?"

"Yes," Eoj answered.

"Ok good," she replied, "that's the biggest ticket in town."

Eoj then told her that the tickets were John's doing and what he was planning on doing.

"I've seen this guy at some of his press conferences, so I think I know where you're going with this. Are you thinking that if he saw the genuine article in person, he just may tone it down a bit?"

"Just a little bit," Eoj said.

Later at the fight, the champion was his usual overconfident and overbearing self. After winning the fight in his usual fashion, his manager came over to Eoj and Michelle and invited them back to the dressing room to meet the champion. It was through him that John made the arrangement, being that they were old friends.

Michelle respectfully declined and told Eoj that she would meet him back at the room.

"Ok love, I won't be long."

Back in the dressing room, the champion was still going on about the fight in his usual way. As his manager and Eoj entered, the room went dead silent and all eyes were on Eoj.

"Ah, hmm," the manager then said as he introduced the men to one another.

"Congratulations on another great victory, champ, you are a true professional," Eoj said.

"Thank you my brother, thank you," he replied, "I really put it on his ass, didn't I?" and before Eoj could respond he went on saying, "I bet his daddy never whupped his ass that bad before."

Eoj again tried to respond and was once again interrupted by the champ saying, "can't nobody beat me, man, nooobody in this world, you hear me?"

Eoj chimed in saying, "No doubt."

"That's right," the champ then said.

Eoj kept speaking while he had the chance, saying, "Hey champ, I know how you like to party so, I want to invite you and a guest to one of the biggest private parties that no one you know has ever heard about or can get into and we'll even provide you transportation to and from, I think there's some V.I.P.s you should meet."

After looking puzzled for a moment, he said, "I'm there, just tell me when."

"In about four months," Eoj said.

"Cool," the champ replied.

Eoj then headed back to his room. While on his way he stepped on a silver dollar in the casino lobby and picked it up and thought to himself, "can I be that lucky?" and headed over to the dollar slots and played it, and for someone who never gambles, Eoj was definitely a lucky man. He hit for 100k and said to himself, "man, that felt good." He couldn't wait to share the news with Michelle so he went right up after collecting and paying off the eagle-eyed tax man.

Back at the room, he shared the news with Michelle and she was ecstatic, saying, "Wow, baby, that's great!! Let's celebrate." "No doubt, let's order something special tonight, what say some lamb chops, caviar, champagne and dessert."

"Works for me, baby."

"Let's do it," Michelle said.

At dinner, Michelle asked, "How did it go with the champ,"

"Fine," Eoj said, "He'll be there."

"I knew he would," Michelle said.

On the jet back home, Eoj gave Michelle the check from the winnings and told her to drop it in the charities account. She was speechless as she gave Eoj a big smile and then managed to whisper, "Ok love," and then gave him a kiss.

Once back from there trip, Eoj and John were meeting more frequently, going over the details of the big event because time was fast approaching. John was telling Eoj, "the only problem that we're having right now is accommodating everyone who wants to come and see your last two fights, so many wants to come and see you for the last and even more wants to see you for the first time so much so that they're more than willing to pay whatever we ask, but that would take a third fight."

"That's not a problem," Eoj said, "let's give them what they want." "Are you sure? because these last three are sure to be the very best of the very worst, I mean these misfits and outcast's will stop at nothing to try and knock you off your throne during your last reign."

"No doubt, looking forward to it. Everything will be cool as long as they oblige the rules. Anyone who even blinks outside the rules will be vanquished immediately. Period."

"Done," John said, "we'll send them a fair warning."

Just as their discussion ended, they saw Michelle driving up to the guest house. They hadn't been there much because of the charity's success, but did come out most weekends to relax, and Eoj still loved going to the track with John.

Michelle came over to the main house to greet the guys and Lisa. They all later had dinner and drinks before he and Michelle called it the night and retired to the guest house.

As they were relaxing, Michelle told Eoj how much she loved the place and all the memories they made there.

"Me too, baby, me too," he said and then he told Michelle there was going to be a third fight for his grand finale."

"Oh, baby," she said, "are you sure you want to do that?" she asked with a sad face.

"Yes, love, it'll be fine and everyone will be happy and it'll be over for once and all."

Michelle then took Eoj by the hand, smiled and said, "No doubt, baby," and Eoj responded, "No doubt, baby."

The big event was only four months from now and Eoj realized he had a huge dilemma on his hands, you see, he's been going to church with Michelle and his future in-laws often and was learning about god's love and what he expected of his people, but at the same time, he knew he had to finish this thing so that he and Michelle could move forward and start their new life together with marriage and start their own family, something he couldn't and wouldn't have as long as he was still fighting.

If ever there was a time for Eoj to be Eoj, it was now literally. He knew if he was ever less than his best in the ring, it would be he that would be vanquished by his enemies and they were more than willing and capable of pulling off such a thing.

Eoj already knew what John Stone would say about his dilemma and he would be right. He would simply say, "Eoj, it's kill or be killed, no if, ands or buts about it."

Eoj felt he needed another positive opinion and Michelle knew what he had to do and was already on board. Eoj wanted to speak to Michelle's father to get an unbiased opinion on the matter, but already knew what had to be done.

He and Michelle planned a dinner with her parents to give Eoj the chance to discuss things with her father. When that day came, it was after dinner when he and Michelle's father discussed things in the living room while Michelle and her mother hung out in the kitchen.

"Is everything ok, son?" Michelle's dad asked Eoj.

Eoj replied, "It will be, I'm sure, I need your advice and opinion on a particular situation because I respect and value what you would have to say, sir."

"Wow, is it that serious, son?" he asked.

"Yes, sir, it is."

"Well, ok, what is it son?"

"I'll have to show you first and then explain to you, dad, you might want to have a seat," and Eoj put a DVD in the player and played it for him, it was his first fight on the dark side.

After watching the DVD he looked as if he just seen a ghost and then got up and made himself a strong drink and offered Eoj the same, then they both sat back down and Eoj started to explain his dilemma and the timing of it and the possible consequences if he didn't go through with what he knew he had to do.

After downing his drink, he said to Eoj, "I'm sure you have Michelle's support, she really loves you, son, we've never seen her happier, and we love you too Eoj and we want see you kids happy and enjoy a healthy and happy life together you've two earned it and deserve nothing less."

"Eoj?" he then asked, "is this the only thing standing in the way of your happiness, son?"

"Yes, sir," Eoj replied.

"Well, son, I can't tell you what to or not to do in this particular situation nor can I condone your killing a man if it winds up going that way, but let me say this, for one to win another must lose and you're no loser son. And sometimes in life we must do things we don't want to do to survive in this life. God bless you, son."

"Thank you, sir, likewise," Eoj replied.

They then shook hands and dad patted him on the back.

Eoj then went into the kitchen to say goodnight to mom and get Michelle so they could leave.

On the way back to the Queens apartment, Michelle asked, "How did it go, babe?"

Eoj smiled and said, "I think it went well, love,"

"That's great," she replied.

Back at the apartment, Eoj opened some champagne and Michelle smiled and asked, "What's the occasion, baby?"

Eoj replied, "We are my queen, we are," "That's right, baby," Michelle said, "Now, tell me what are you going to do with me for the rest of the night?"

"Well first, I'd love to have some dessert."

"Ok," she said.

"I'd love to take you to paradise even better,"

She said, "I was hoping you would say that, lover."

The next day, they started going over their plans for their new life together, starting with leaving for a short vacation the night of the last fight, destination? a well-deserved surprise, a house close to mom, dad, and children.

The start of the three fight finale was just a week away and Michelle could barely contain her excitement, she knew this would soon be over and Eoj was signing dozens of his special 8's for John to give as gifts to some special friends of his during the last three fights.

After signing the gloves, Eoj made himself a drink and then took his world championship belt out of its travel case and stared at it, studying it, every gem stone, every inscription and its meaning, all the precious metals and its significant weight.

Just then Michelle walked into the room and asked, "May I join you?" and Eoj said, "Please."

She then sat next to him on the sofa and said, "Wow, every time I see it, it seems like there's something new on it."

"I was just thinking the same," Eoj said.

Michelle then said, "This belt fits you perfectly, my king."

Eoj replied, "On the contrary, it's you who fits me perfectly, my queen, I would have kept falling deeper into the abyss if it wasn't for you, babe, your love and kindness, caring words and tender touch and patience are a gift, simply put sweetheart your love is all I'll ever need."

Michelle responded with a smile and a tear as they embraced.

It's fight night, the lights are bright, the crowd is loud and the place is electric.

Eoj chose the ring to be black and gold for his final three fights, the colors spoke for themselves. Standing in the ring, his opponent in the ring, this 300lb, 6'3, mountain of a man that goes by the moniker (the Siberian iceman) is grooving to the tune of (Another One Bites the Dust) by the group Queen. He has a reputation for bone-breaking body shots and jaw-crushing jabs that are unreal.

The crowd has gotten louder as Eoj entered the arena, grooving to the tune (We Are the Champions) by the same group and wearing his sinister smile. Michelle was sitting front row center to support the 'one true love of her life' as she likes to refer to him as. And when John saw Eoj, he thought to himself, "Damn, this is going to be something tonight."

When Eoj spotted Michelle and they made eye contact, he then saluted her and pounded his chest a few times with one of his super 8s to show he was more than ready to go. She then smiled and nodded her head.

The bell sounded to start the first round and instantly, Eoj brought the madness to the big man and delivered a gang of thunderous head and body shots which were so vicious, they left the big guy bleeding profusely from the face and mouth, and even the bruises on his body started to drip blood.

Eoj's dark talents were in rare form this night, not allowing the big guy to land a single punch and every time he tried, it was met with a bomb from Eoj's arsenal.

The bell sounded to end the first round and while Eoj was standing alone in his corner, he noticed a commotion breaking out in the iceman's corner, his handlers were yelling at him and kept throwing water in his face in a nasty way. Suddenly the frustrated beast stood up and punched one of the men off the ring apron leaving him unconscious on the floor and just as he went after a second handler the bell sounded to start the second round.

Still bleeding, frustrated and not sure what to do next, the iceman with rage in his eyes standing center ring just started to stare at Eoj and in an instant was dropped by a vicious doubled-up right hand.

As the iceman got up slowly, Eoj knew it was time to shut him down and he did just that as they were standing face-to-face and in a blink of an eye, the iceman was down again and not even trying to get up, falling victim to Eoj's phantom punch nicknamed "speed kills", if you're not focused, you'll never see it coming and even when you're focused you'll never see it coming, hence "speed kills".

Later that night, at the main house during dinner, John said to Eoj, "You, sir, never cease to amaze me, that was fast, fierce, and flawless, an absolute master piece. We are definitely going out like the 4th of July."

"No doubt," Eoj responded.

John and Michelle raised their glasses to Eoj and they all toasted to "no doubt". John then revealed to Eoj that his take for the night was 5 million and his bonus was 75k cash.

Eoj responded, "That's good stuff, man, thanks."

"No doubt," John said as they all shared a short laugh.

John then said to Eoj, "I really thought you were going to kill the Iceman tonight, being that the ring was dressed in black and gold."

"I did," Eoj said, "just not in the physical way, it was more of a mental kill. I killed his anger and confidence, therefore rendering him useless to his purpose."

"I see," John said.

Eoj and Michelle called it the night and headed to the guest house. Once there, Michelle released her happiness saying, "When did you know you weren't going to kill that guy? And I'm so glad you didn't have to, what you did was so much better, baby."

"Thanks, sweetheart, I'm happy about the outcome also. Hey, what say we have some dessert and then maybe we can go—?" Just then Michelle interrupted and said, "Absolutely," with a smile on her face.

The next morning, they headed back to Queens to relax and finish going over their plans.

Back at the apartment Michelle got a call, it was her father and he wanted to talk to Eoj, so she handed him the phone and mouthed to him, "It's dad," as he took the phone from her, he winked at her and smiled.

"Hey dad," he then said, "How are you, sir?"

After a few minutes of explaining to him that he found an alternate route for getting his mission done, Michelle's father then said, "You see how prayer changes things, my son?"

"Yes, sir," Eoj responded, "thank you for your prayers, dad." They then hung up and gave Michelle back her phone and said,

"Wow."

Michelle then asked, "Was everything ok?"

Eoj responded, "Everything is just great, my love, just great."

Eoj then informed Michelle that he had to run some errands. "Ok, baby, you want to use my car? I'm not going anywhere today."

"That would be great, babe, thanks," as she gave him the key, they kissed and embraced then Eoj was on his way.

Little did Michelle know that he was on his way to pick out her engagement ring so that he could propose to her in London Paris, the night of his last fight. And thanks to her parents, he was able to get all the info he needed to make it a perfect night, info like her ring size, etc.

As Eoj entered the apartment, Michelle was putting the finishing touches on dinner, and she had champagne on ice. Eoj asked, "What's the occasion?"

She said, "We are, baby, we are," with a smile on her face.

Eoj responded, "That's right, my love."

At the table, it was more than obvious they both had something on their minds.

They then look at each other, Michelle with tears in her eyes and Eoj with tears welling up in his, they both smiled and Eoj said, "What is it, baby."

Michelle said, "I just can't believe how happy I am and how happy we're going to be together, baby."

"Oh my god, this is crazy, I honestly was thinking the same thing," said Eoj.

Michelle then said, "Honey, do you mind if we come back to the dinner a little later because right now I just really need you, love."

"No doubt," Eoj said and Michelle did her usual thing and they went to the bedroom.

The next morning, Eoj got a call from John, he wanted to know which of Eoj's last two fights did he want the current champion to come to. Eoj replied, "Have him come to the finale."

"Ok, good," John said and then asked how was everything.

"Fine," said Eoj, "It just feels surreal at times, I'm finally getting everything I need and want in life and I can't help but feel there's some negative force at work to try and sabotage my happiness and I'll never let that happen, I swear it on my life."

"Hey, Eoj," John said, "We both know that'll never happen and for those who don't, they will have to find out the hard way."

Eoj then asked John how things were going in Paris. John said, "You're all set, you guys are going to have a great time and congratulations in advance on your engagement."

"Thanks, man, two more fights and we'll be straight."

"Damn straight," and then hung up.

As Eoj and Michelle were having breakfast, he handed her his 75k bonus from the fight and told her it was for the charity, and before she could say anything, he asked her, "Does the charity need anything else?"

Michelle said, "No, baby, we're doing just fine, actually, we're ahead on some of our projects."

"That's great," said Eoj, "We've come a long way, love."

The second fight was only days away and they just decided to spend their time together relaxing and enjoying each other's company.

It's fight night and the arena is filled with local and international guests, most seeing Eoj for the first time. The crowd was more than lively and John, with a grin on his face, thought to himself, "This never gets old."

Michelle was front and center in her seat and dressed in a stunning black and gold pant and jacket suit, matching the ring and Eoj's trunks and special 8s gloves. And speaking of special 8s, Eoj spotted John handing out some of the gloves John had him sign weeks ago for this particular occasion and the recipients couldn't be happier, for the gloves were a rare commodity.

Eoj's challenger tonight is a nightmare straight from hell and weighing in at an eye-popping 350lbs and standing 6′4, this hulk of a man was covered in scars and tattoos and his flesh was red literally, and going by the moniker Devil's Advocate (DA) for short. When John Stone saw this thing, he thought to himself, "This guy is much scarier in real life." Michelle's response was, "Oh god," and as Eoj entered the ring and upon seeing the behemoth for the first time, he uttered the words, "What the—," must have been the red flesh.

As security was relieving Eoj of his belt, he and Michelle made eye contact and Eoj had to do a double take after seeing her in that stunning outfit, the last time he saw her, she was wearing a bath robe and a smile. He then smiled and saluted her and she smiled back and nodded her head.

As they waited for the bell to sound, Eoj focused on his game plan of taking the big guy for a long and painful swim before dismantling him.

The bell sounds to start the first round, and as they met center ring, and as Eoj looked him in the eyes, he noticed immediately there was no one home and didn't hesitate to fire off the first shots, a classic one-two combo to the face with speed and power costing the big guy two teeth and his mouthpiece. That seemed to get his attention. He then let out a frustrated scream and charged Eoj to no avail, being dropped by a ballistic of a right hand and spitting out blood.

As he slowly gets back up, Eoj instantly lay into him with some body bombs which he tolerated quite well.

As the bell sounds to end the first round, Eoj turns and heads to his vacant corner, but the big guy doesn't do the same. Instead, he waits for Eoj to turn his back and decides to take a cheap shot at Eoj, and just as he starts to make his move, Michelle drops her drink and calls out to Eoj, just in time as he turns around and ducks a tremendous right that spins the big guy around, and would have been totally devastating for Eoj had he not reacted in time, and thanks to Michelle he did.

By now, DA's team was in the ring, dragging and pushing him back to his corner, but the line had already been crossed and as a hush came over the crowd, Eoj's security team was waiting for him to give the word of life or death.

Eoj's eyes were red with rage as he watched Michelle with tears streaming down her face. Knowing how upset she must have been, Eoj saluted her again and blew her a kiss and she returned it.

Eoj then declined to have the big guy taken out by security, and also sent Michelle a message asking if she wanted to wait for him in the dressing room, and her message back to him was:

"Absolutely not. I'm here for you, my king, and will never leave your side no matter what, my love. Make him pay."

And with that Eoj became enraged and unloaded his arsenal of dark talents on the big guy and letting his darkness shine as he prepared DA for his trip back to hell.

As DA was about to take his fall to the canvas for the last time, Eoj held him up and pushed him into the corner and delivered some devastating exclamation points to the body before letting him take that final plunge to the canvas.

It was done.

John Stone and Michelle both breathed a sigh of relief as they rushed to meet Eoj in the dressing room.

Once there, Eoj picked Michelle up in a loving embrace as they kissed and with a smile on his face, he whispered to her, "Just one more, baby."

John then shook his hand and said, "Well done, sir."

"No doubt," said Eoj, "Give me about 20 mins and I will greet your guest."

"Thanks," said John, "I'll see you out there."

After hitting the shower, he and Michelle went back out to the arena to greet John's special guests. They seemed to be glowing as they entered the arena, everyone could tell there was something so special about them, a true power couple.

Eoj met and had small talk with the guests that John gave a pair of Eoj's special 8s to.

A little later that night, back at the main house, John, Eoj, and Michelle were having drinks and dessert when John announced that he had some great news to share with Eoj and Michelle, as they both looked at John.

Michelle smiled and said, "We're always ready for great news."

Eoj chimed in, "No doubt."

John then said, "Eoj, we've accomplished our mission as of tonight and everything from the finale is going to be a bonus, and speaking of bonuses, your package is waiting for you at the guest house, now you guys have a good night, seems you have some celebrating to do."

"No doubt," Eoj said as he and Michelle left.

Once they were back at the guest house, Michelle made him his favorite drink and sat up on the sofa, waiting for Eoj to bring her up to speed on what John Stone said and meant by it.

"Ok, my queen, we now have so many blessings bestowed upon us, it's hard to keep count. We can now retire together and start our new life as we discussed, for we now have a permanent residual income that will help our dreams come true, love. We can only grow from here."

Michelle wept softly and Eoj asked, "What's wrong baby?"

She responded, "Nothing's wrong, baby, everything has never been so right in my life. These are pure tears of happiness. I'm speechless."

"Well, you don't have to say anything, sweetheart, we can just quietly enjoy it for now."

Eoj then opened one of 2 envelopes containing 100k each, one was his night's bonus, the other was John's dollar-for-dollar matching contribution.

Eoj's take for the night was 10 million.

Eoj then suddenly became speechless and joined Michelle on the sofa, where they embraced while listening to some soft romantic music before calling it a night.

The next morning at the breakfast table, Eoj said to Michelle, "I want to show you the gift we got for mom and dad."

"We did?" asked Michelle.

"We certainly did," said Eoj and handed her an envelope. She smiled and opened it, and to her surprise, it was their mortgage paid in full.

Michelle said, "OMG!!! The love just keeps on coming," as she wiped her eyes.

"Yes, that's what love does, baby, you taught me that."

Michelle said, "I think it's your happiness that's bringing out the best in you, love."

Eoj said, "I think you're right, cause you're my happiness, you're my everything, baby."

Michelle then said, "Baby, what you're doing for my parents is tremendous and—"

Eoj interrupted her saying, "We, it's 'we', baby, now and always."

She apologized and said, "I also think that we shouldn't forget about your siblings, baby, although you don't get along so well right now."

Eoj looked at her for a moment and responded, "No doubt, we'll just have to figure out how to do that."

"Ok, baby, let's," Michelle said and gave him a kiss.

"Let's make dinner plans with mom and dad so we can give them their gift, I can't wait to see their faces when we give them their gift."

"Wow, someone sounds excited."

"I am," Eoj said.

"Well, just how excited are you, bad boy?" Michelle asked with a little smile on her face.

Eoj then said, "Well, baby, you know my actions speak louder than my words, so I'll just have to show you."

Michelle then said, "Well, I'm waiting, bad boy," then Eoj took her by the hand and led her to the bedroom.

Tonight they're having dinner at Michelle's parent's house to give them their gift and share some great news with them also.

On the way there, they stopped to pick up some champagne and a bouquet of flowers for the special occasion.

As they drove up the drive way, mom and dad were sitting on the deck enjoying the weather. As they got up to greet them, Michelle handed her mother the flowers and said, "These are for you, mom."

"Oh, thank you, baby," she responded.

Her dad then said, "When are you going to give me that car, girl?"

Michelle then said, "We have something better for you guys."

Eoj chimed in saying, "No doubt."

Her father then asked, "Really?" as they all went inside the house.

"Can I get you a drink, son?" he asked Eoj.

"Yes, thanks."

"Your usual."

"Yes, sir."

As they all sat and engaged in small talk, mom announced that she would be serving one of Eoj's favorites, being that he was from Louisiana, gumbo and homemade sweet corn bread.

Eoj said, "Whoa, how did you know, mom," and she just looked at Michelle and smiled.

"Well, thank you, ladies, I look forward to it."

"Me too," said dad and they all laughed.

At the table, dad gave grace as they enjoyed the special meal which coincidentally would turn out to be a very special day for the whole family.

During the dessert phase, Eoj and Michelle announced that they had a very special gift for two very special people in their lives and proposed a toast to mom and dad.

Eoj then said, "Here's to God's love and family, the two things you, mom and dad, represent well," and Michelle with a tear streaming down her cheek said, "Amen."

She and Eoj then handed them a gold envelope with a smiley face on it and said, "Thanks for all you do, we love you guys."

By now the ladies were crying and dad and Eoj were fighting back their tears.

As they opened the envelope and saw their mortgage stamped 'paid in full', mom and dad both sat back down and said, "Hallelujah, thank you, Jesus," with tears streaming down their faces.

At that point, Eoj picked up his drink and went out on the deck to avoid showing his emotions.

After a few moments, Michelle and her parents came out to see Eoj. Mom and dad gave him a hug and said, "Thank you so much, son."

They all sat down on the deck and Eoj said, "There's more. Michelle and I are retiring after my last order of business in about a week from now and we'll have all the time we need to be a family."

"This is a glorious blessing," said Michelle's mother.

"It sure is," said her father.

As they were leaving, Michelle and her parents were in a group hug and Eoj said, "We'll see you guys soon."

In the car, Eoj said to Michelle, "Let's stay in Queens for a few days."

Michelle smiled and said, "Sounds great, babe."

Once at the apartment, she said to Eoj, "Thanks for one of the best days of my life, baby, I've never seen my parents happier, I can't explain how much of a load we took off their shoulders."

Eoj said, "Well they more than deserve it, sweetheart, and it was a pleasure to be a part of helping them out."

"I love you, Eoj."

"And I love you, baby," he replied.

Later that night, Eoj was sitting on the sofa drink in hand and looking over his championship belt, reminiscing about how he got to this point in his life, from being a poor fearless kid from Brooklyn NY and taking on unrelenting abuse from family and strangers, to flipping the script on bullies, punishing the punishers, to advocating for those in need through his and Michelle's charities and generosity, and finding his one true love, the woman of his dreams, and in the end he gets to start life again.

He then thought to himself, "This has to be destiny," because he could never be that lucky.

Just as he came to the end of his thoughts, he got a call from John Stone letting him know that everything for the finale was all set and that the current champion was still quite excited to come.

"That's good," Eoj said.

"I'll be there in a couple of days and we can go over the details, I'll see you when you get here, sir," responded John Stone.

As he hung up the phone he looked up to find Michelle standing in the doorway in a very sexy and tasteful lingerie outfit in one of Eoj's favorite colors, emerald green.

"Oh, I'm loving this," he said as he looked her over.

Michelle then said in a soft voice, "Hey, my champion, may I have a word with you?"

"No doubt," Eoj said and Michelle giggled and took him by the hand and led him to the bedroom.

The next morning while having breakfast, Michelle smiled at Eoj and asked what had gotten into him last night.

"Just the beast you brought out of me, you sexy lady."

"Why, thank you," Michelle said.

"On the contrary," Eoj said as they both smiled and held hands. Eoj then asked Michelle if she had a problem going back to the estate today.

She responded, "Not at all baby, I have nothing doing until we get back from vacation."

Later as they arrived, they noticed there was a lot of activity on the grounds. "Is this all part of the finale?" Michelle asked.

"Oh yeah," said Eoj, "We're going out like the fourth of July, baby, with all the works."

"Wow, I can hardly wait," she then asked, "How are you feeling baby?"

"Oh, I'm good love, I'm so good."

They then went into the main house to greet John, they hadn't seen Lisa in quite some time, which could only mean one thing, they wouldn't be seeing her again.

Once inside, they greeted John and chatted for a few minutes before Michelle excused herself so the men could talk business.

As they went over the plans, John told Eoj about the award winning chefs that were doing the barbecue and the pros that were doing the fireworks on the barge, to the three bars and the dance floor and etc.

"Man, this is going to be the party to beat," exclaimed Eoj.

"Yes, it is," said John Stone, he then said, I've got to tell ya, I'm honored to be a part of so many celebrations all rolled up in one, we have a double retirement, a new home, an engagement, a prosperous partnership, tell me, did I leave anything out."

"No, I think you pretty much covered everything," Eoj said as they both laughed.

John then said, "We've come a long way, my friend, and after this chapter, we'll continue to go even further."

"No doubt," Eoj responded as they shook hands. John then said to Eoj, "I do have a couple more surprises for you guys, but they'll have to wait till fight night."

"Cool, can't wait," said Eoj. Eoj then went back to the guest house to relax with Michelle.

As he came through the door, she ran to embrace him and then asked, "What do you want to do for dinner baby?"

"Well, I actually feel like Chinese and some dessert." "Ok, that sounds good," Michelle said.

After relaxing for a couple of days it was fight night. The arena was a spectacle like Oscar night in Hollywood, but there are no actors here, not one, instead, you have a stage showcasing the most profound violence on the dark side of sports, where losers most times die and winners thrive with cash and the other man's prize, where madness runs rampant and spilled blood is all too common to see, and depending on your tolerance, you'll realize you're either at fight night or fright night.

Eoj was in his dressing room relaxing, having a drink and listening to his smooth R&B as John and Michelle came in to check on him before he took that walk into utter uncertainty to face his most formidable foe yet. Michelle gave him a long and hard embrace and said, "I love you, baby."

Eoj kissed her on the forehead and said, "I'll see you out there," with a smile. Michelle smiled back as she left.

John then said, "Congratulations, champ."

"Thank you, sir," Eoj responded. "Speaking of champs, where is our friend?" Eoj asked John.

"I put him and his lady friend ring side, you can't miss him and he definitely won't miss you."

"Cool," Eoj said.

"See you out there," John said as he left. "No doubt," Eoj responded and saluted John.

A moment later, Eoj heard the arena erupt in cheers and knew it was show time and headed to the ring, no music for Eoj tonight, he was locked, loaded, and focused on the task at hand.

As he approached the ring he could see the current champion looking over his belt that he had the security team bring over with a verbal message. He was already in a state of shock from the belt alone and then the message was relayed to him saying, stick around and see how it's done. And as they took the belt and left, he looked up just in time to see Eoj entering the ring and was floored. He looked at Eoj in shock and awe.

Eoj was wearing his sinister grin and gave a head nod. His foe tonight is a solid 340lb, 6 ft half-breed representing Samoa and Japan and is a former sumo wrestler who's been known to punch open some of his heavy bags and goes by the moniker (COC) crack on crack. This guy loves his drugs and suffers from anger and mental issues, the perfect storm of madness and violence.

As the men were waiting for the bell to sound the start of the first round, an earie silence came over the arena, Eoj was no stranger to this type of thing, it just told him there were other forces at work here, John had seen this before at one of Eoj's fights' but wasn't concerned, Michelle on the other hand hadn't seen anything like this before and grew concerned that her and Eoj's dreams may not come to fruition. As she looked up at Eoj with a tear streaming down her cheek, he smiled then saluted and blew her a kiss, and at that very moment, she knew everything would be alright, for with his super natural talents, he was also a force to be reckoned with.

Most of the spectators felt they were about to witness a true clash of the titans. The current champion grew a little anxious to see what kind of talents would earn someone such a belt as Eoj's.

The bell sounded to start the first round and the two warriors met center ring and immediately started throwing bombs at one another, neither would back down and the bomb throwing tirade lasted the entire round.

While waiting for round two, Eoj learned all he needed to know about (COC) to advance himself to the victory that awaited his and Michelle's new life together and absolutely nothing was going to stop it.

The bell sounded to start the second round and they met center ring again and in an instant, Eoj fired off two vicious jabs that busted the big guy's nose and lips open, Eoj had drew first blood and was just getting started. Eoj knew the big guy was too slow to land any punches face to face, so he continued to pepper him with those flesh ripping jabs and whenever the big guy took a swing, Eoj would side step him and lay into his body with the heavy artillery.

The big guy started to realize that if he had any hope of beating Eoj he had his work cut out for him, the bell sounded to end round two and as Eoj returned to his vacant corner.

The current champion took notice and didn't know what to make of it, Eoj was just calmly standing there as if he was waiting for the very first round to start.

It is now the fifth round and the big guy is starting to talk to himself and keeps repeating the same strategy that hasn't worked for him since round one. By now Eoj had administered enough punishment that would have finished off any of his most deadly and ruthless opponents. Just as Eoj started to ponder why the big guy was still standing after hitting him with a bomb of a kidney shot, the big guy repeatedly asked Eoj, "Are you death? are you death?" And Eoj realized the madness was starting to kick in from all the dope in the big guy's system, Eoj then hit him with another kill shot to the head and finally the big guy goes down to one knee and as the ref starts the 8 count and Eoj heads to the neutral corner, the big guy gets up and pushes the ref out of the way and yells to Eoj, "Oh death, where is thy sting?" and in an instant, Eoj rushed over and dropped him with a mighty right hand and with this you could hear the big guy start to snore.

Michelle breathed a sigh relief and the arena erupted wildly in applause, cheers, and whistles. Eoj then took a bow as the current champion waved to him. As Eoj made his way back to the dressing room, he was happy to see that Michelle had beat him there and embraced him as he came in, with tears of joy in her eyes she thanked him for the happiest night of her life. Eoj then said to her, "The night is still young, my queen, the night is still young and there's so much more to come," "Tonight," She said. "Yes, love," he said.

John Stone entered the room with a big grin on his face and said, "Damn, Eoj, this is my favorite masterpiece."

"Mine too," said Eoj.

"Mine three," Michelle chimed in as they all smiled.

John then asked Eoj, "How long can you stay before you have to leave?"

"Leave?" Michelle asked, "are we going somewhere tonight, baby?"

"Yes," Eoj said, "and you're going to love it, I promise." "Wow, I like that," she said.

Eoj then told John, "As soon as they can get the jet ready, well, you have at least an hour then," John said, "So let's go mingle for a few and enjoy some great barbecue and the fireworks and so I can also share my surprises for you guys."

"Let's do it," Eoj said, "I'll see you out there in 20 minutes."

"See you out there, champ," John said as he left.

Eoj then hit the shower as Michelle waited for him.

The first person they greeted was the current champion, and all he wanted to do was thank Eoj for the lesson and apologize for his behavior, saying to Eoj, "You, sir, are no doubt, the true heavy weight champion of the world, you have taken what I could never take and given what I would never be able to give in that ring, that was truly supernatural and thanks for giving me a chance to bare witness, Sir, not meaning to be rude but—"Eoj then interrupted him and said, "No I don't mind—it's ten million."

"Wow, no wonder I couldn't take my eyes off it or my hands for that matter." He and Eoj shared a brief laugh as they wished each other a good night.

He and Michelle was enjoying some barbecue and the festivities when John finally came over to share his surprises with them, "First, let me say congrats on everything, guys. Eoj, first thing is, we have a new G5 that was delivered a few days ago that you guys are going to use for your trip tonight, second, your take for tonight is 10 million and your bonus is 1 million and you retire with the belt and we insured it for 12. Now, you guys go and enjoy your well deserved vacation and I'll see you guys when you get back. Oh—" John then said, "one more thing, your other surprise will be waiting for you there at brunch tomorrow," as he left them at their table.

Eoj then asked Michelle if she was ready to leave, she said, "but honey, I didn't pack anything." Eoj then said, "Oh, don't worry, sweetheart, we'll get what we need when we get there."

"Well, baby, I guess I'm ready then."

On the jet, Michelle said to Eoj you look so tired baby, I'm too happy to be tired, as she handed him a drink and sat in his lap.

"Wow, you really pulled in some major cash tonight, sir," she said."

"No, love we did because we are a team and there's no I in team but just like We there is an e."

"I'm sorry, baby, I'm still trying to get used to calling your things our things because it's so much."

"We're going to have to work on that, my queen."

"Hey we still have plenty of time before we get to our destination what say we lay down and listen to some nice soft music and relax a bit."

"Love to, but where are we going to lay, baby?"

Eoj then walked over to the sofa and pushed the button on the side of it and it converted into a bed and he then smiled at her, and she said, "Nice," and then walked over while Eoj got pillows from an overhead compartment.

They laid down and fell asleep almost instantly. After a while, the intercom phone rang and it was the captain notifying them that they would be landing in Paris France shortly.

It was one of Michelle's favorite places in the world and as she hung up the intercom, she gently woke Eoj and whispered to him that they were about to land and as he sat in his seat and strapped himself in, he noticed Michelle smiling at him and he asked what, and Michelle asked, "What are you up to, bad boy?"

Eoj winked at her and just smiled at her leaving it a complete mystery.

As they arrived at the hotel, Michelle was taken by the sights of Paris at night. Once in their suite, Eoj said, "Wow, it's so beautiful and were right by the Eiffel tower, we should take a short walk before we call it the night," "Yes," said Michelle excitedly, "Let's go."

As they were leaving the hotel, Eoj waved at the front desk which was a signal, he arranged for the staff to go up and prepare the suite for the celebration he planned for himself and Michelle.

As they were walking, Michelle said, "Oh, baby, I can't believe we're really here, oh, I so love this place."

As they got to the tower, they noticed a small crowd and there were musicians playing a romantic tune and there were about a dozen large bouquets of red roses and everyone seem to have a glass of champagne and a moment later, a couple handed Eoj and Michelle a couple of glasses, and as they poured the champagne, Michelle asked, "What's the occasion?" and the couple then pointed to Eoj who was on bended knee right behind her showcasing a five carat princess cut diamond ring.

As Michelle slowly turned and saw Eoj, he said, "My one and only true love, complete me and marry me, my queen." Michelle said, "Yes, my one and only true love, my king." The crowd applauded and toast to their happiness.

As they walked back to the hotel, they were holding hands and they were still shedding tears of joy. As they walked past the front desk, the gentleman behind the desk gave Eoj a head nod, signaling that everything was all set for them in the suite.

As they entered the suite, Michelle cried out, "Oh, baby, oh my god, look at all of this," and then embraced him and said, "If this is a dream, please, don't wake me." "Well, baby, it's a dream, it's our dream come true," Eoj said.

There was a great spread set up for them, a custom made cake decorated with hearts and roses and the inscription: "Eoj and Michelle, a timeless love story," champagne and caviar, etc. And in the master bath, there was a path of rose petals leading to the huge bubble bath that awaited them.

After enjoying themselves at the table, they took the champagne and the celebration into the master bath and enjoyed some soft lighting and soft music while they relaxed in that huge bubble bath. After they enjoyed the bath, they headed towards the bed. Eoj then asked Michelle, "Want to hear what I learned in French today?"

"Sure, let's hear it," she said. And in French, he said, "Now it's time to enjoy the cream of the crop." Michelle spoke some French and smiled, saying, "It sure is, lover."

It was late morning when they got up and Eoj suggested that they stay in and relax after such a whirlwind day the day before. Michelle agreed and a moment later, the room phone rang; it was the front desk informing them that they had lunch reservations courtesy of Mr. John Stone.

As Eoj hung up the phone, he informed Michelle and said, "That must be the surprise he was talking about." "Ok, baby, we can do it. What time is lunch and where?" "One," Eoj said, "and it's at the restaurant in the lobby." "Good, we can relax for a while longer, sweetheart, we can both use it," Michelle said.

"Me more than you, you're an animal, woman," Eoj said with a smile. "Me?! Me!" Michelle then said, "I couldn't help it, besides I was just showing you how happy I was, baby." "Wow," Eoj said, "You are one happy lady, baby!! And I plan on keeping you that way, love." "And I you," Michelle said.

It was that time and they headed down for lunch and stopped at the entrance of the restaurant, and as they were being shown to their table, Michelle heard a very familiar laugh as they approached their table and thought to herself that can't be right, that can't be mom, but when they got to the table it was mom and dad and Michelle nearly fainted and Eoj quickly held her up and helped her to her seat.

As she regained her composure she said, "Oh my god I can't believe this," she said as she was still looking shock, confused, and happy all at once. "Nice to see you too," her parents said with big smiles on their faces.

Eoj took her hand and said, "Sweetheart, I forgot to mention that I'm also a master of great surprises." "I can see that," she said as she got back up to greet her parents. As she embraced them she and her mother started to cry, and her mother said to her, "It's ok, baby, it's ok."

They then sat back down and Eoj handed her his handkerchief, and as she started to wipe her tears, her parents took notice of the ring and her mother said in a loud voice, "Goodness." Michelle was a little embarrassed and said, "Mom, please." Then her dad chimed in and said, "Whoa, is that a flash light?" and Eoj couldn't help but laugh.

Eoj then asked them how their flight was on the G5 and dad said, "Wow, son, I can easily get used to that, I almost didn't know how to act, I mean popcorn, drinks, movies, and snacks and sitting in a big ol recliner, man, I was in heaven among the heavens. Thank you, son."

And mom said, "Yes, thank you, baby, it was the best flight I've ever had." Michelle was smiling and still glowing from all the happiness that had recently descended upon her and Eoj. She then asked her parents where they were staying and mom said, "Oh just down the hall from you guys."

She then looked at Eoj and he smiled and said, "Surprise." She then smiled back and said, "You are too much." They all spent the next week in Paris, celebrating all their blessings and enjoying all the good things Paris had to offer before heading back to the states and their newly blessed lives.

It was time to leave Paris and as they were about to board the G5, they all paused to take one good last look at Paris. Eoj noticed the long faces everyone had on and said, "Don't worry guys we'll be back." That seemed to bring back the smiles they had lost and they boarded the plane.

Dad and Eoj sat on the sofa and shared conversation and watched sports, mom and Michelle were in the captain chairs at the table talking and having their fun. Dad then asked Eoj if he thought he would ever miss the fight game. Eoj answer was a profound, "Yes," and dad looked shocked. He then said, "But not enough to ever go back to it." Dad then smiled and said, "Amen to that."

Once back, there was a limo waiting for them. Eoj and Michelle dropped mom and dad off first before heading back to their apartment in Queens. As they said their goodbyes, mom and dad expressed how they couldn't wait to see them at the upcoming house blessing for their new home.

Back at the apartment, as they were relaxing, Michelle said to Eoj, "Hey, baby, tell me something, how in the world did you ever manage to pull it all off?" "I had a lot of help, baby, from mom and dad and John and between us, we were able to get it done, love."

"Well, thanks to all of you, I got the engagement of my dreams. Thank you, baby." "You're welcome, sweetheart," said Eoj.

Later that day, Eoj called up John Stone to thank him for helping everything go as well as it did. John was happy to hear from Eoj and as they discussed things, he informed Eoj that the current champion sent V.I.P. tickets for him, Eoj, and guest to his next title fight coming up in Vegas.

"I think he just wants to return the favor," John said. "Sounds good, I'd love to go," said Eoj. "How are you enjoying retirement so far?" John asked. "Great," said Eoj, "we're happy and busy and all is going well." "As it should," said John.

As time passed things continued to grow for them all, their relationships, partnership as well as the charities. It was one beautiful spring day when Michelle announced to Eoj that he was going to make a great father. She then informed him that god had gifted them another blessing, a little one on the way. Eoj then jumped out of bed excitedly and asked, "Really, sweetheart?" and she then showed him the positive reading from the pregnancy test. They then embraced and gave god thanks. Eoj then said to Michelle as she smiled, "I love our life."

THE END